2 nd

PADDLING BASICS
Canoeing

PADDLING BASICS
Canoeing

Cecil Kuhne

Illustrations by Cherie Kuhne

STACKPOLE
BOOKS

Published by
STACKPOLE BOOKS
5067 Ritter Road
Mechanicsburg, PA 17055

Printed in The United States of America

10 9 8 7 6 5 4 3 2 1

First edition

Library of Congress Cataloging-in-Publication Data
Kuhne, Cecil, 1952-
      Canoeing / Cecil Kuhne : illustrations by Cherie Kuhne. — 1st ed.
      p. cm. — (Paddling basics)
      Includes bibliographical references.
      ISBN 0-8117-2881-1 (pbk)
      1. Canoes and canoeing.   I. Kuhne, Cherie.   II. Title
III. Series: Kuhne, Cecil, 1952-   Paddling basics.
GV783.K79   1998   97-24514
797.1′22—dc21   CIP

To my paddling friends at Nantahala Outdoor Center

CONTENTS

ACKNOWLEDGMENTS

No book is the work of a single person, and this one is certainly no exception. I owe much to the kind and proficient editors at Stackpole Books: David Uhler, for coming up with the idea; Mark Allison, for directing the project, and Dave Richwine, for his editorial expertise.

My friends at Nantahala Outdoor Center were, as always, pivotal in keeping my enthusiasm for paddling high, and for being an inspiration in many ways they'll never know. Likewise the editors at *Canoe & Kayak* magazine, where I am proud to serve as contributing editor.

And lastly, but most importantly, I am indebted to my wife, Cherie, for her quiet encouragement and for her magnificent drawings.

INTRODUCTION

We slipped our canoes into the clear, warm waters that would be the object of our pursuit for the next several days. The jade green stream was calm and glassy here, and the boats swished their wakes so cleanly across the surface that the water seemed to crack with the intrusion.

We found ourselves in the enviable position of paddling a resplendent stream through that jagged plateau known as the Ozarks. It was a place of dense forest, steep valleys, imposing bluffs, mysterious caves, and most impressive of all—clear, rushing springs. Spewing from the earth, these cascades are impressive not only for their limitless abundance, but also for their extreme purity. As they chatter noisily over polished boulders, they join together to become rivers ideal for canoeing.

Even today, this region of rugged beauty remains isolated. The scenery is extremely varied: precipitous cliffs, shimmering gravel bars, rolling pastures, sloping woodlands. Forests of oak and hickory abound, mixed with stands of birch and willow. Old sycamores spread their shade under a dense canopy. Watercress thrives where springs gush from cracks in the limestone.

The camaraderie that developed among us on that wilderness wandering was especially memorable. Spending long days sharing new adventures in spectacular surroundings had a way of bringing people together. Even now, we talk about the trip that occurred years ago.

The aim of this book is to enable—and, I hope, encourage—you to enter this splendid realm. Its modest goal is to show those new to the sport of canoeing some of the basic principles about the boat, its accessories, paddling strokes, maneuvering techniques, and safety concerns. But no book, no matter how good, can replace that of hands-on, on-the-water teaching by an expert instructor. For that, I encourage you to seek the assistance of a renowned paddling school like Nantahala Outdoor Center or a local canoe club. There you'll experience practical, real-world situations. Better yet, you'll meet like-minded souls whose camaraderie is clearly much of the reason to be out there in the first place.

My wish is that your experiences will be as meaningful as mine and countless others' who have dipped a paddle over the millennia—which brings me to canoeing's timeless appeal. Despite changes in materials and refinements in design, the canoe is basically the same craft that it was hundreds of years ago. It will, no doubt, have its share of advancements in the future. But centuries from now, when technology has made inconceivable strides, our descendants will still be paddling a boat very similar to the one you are now paddling.

There are very, very few things you can say that about.

1

The Boat

The canoe is one of those inspired designs—elegant, efficient, simple, adaptable. It is sleek enough to glide easily through water, yet capable of hauling heavy loads; it is maneuverable in whitewater, yet able to hold a straight line in the wind; it is rugged enough to withstand abuse, yet light enough to be portaged. It is, in short, a creation perfectly suited to its place and purpose.

For these reasons, the canoe incites almost religious devotion among its followers. The reasons for such affection are easy to grasp. Watch a canoe slice its way across a broad expanse of lake one day, and then negotiate the tortured turns of rock-studded whitewater the next, and you will quickly understand.

Though simple in concept, canoes are available in an amazingly wide array of designs and materials. Yet all of them have a few basic features in common. All canoes, for example, have a hull, which is simply the outside form of the boat. The hull can be made from a variety of materials ranging from wood to plastic. The bow, of course, is the front of the boat, and the stern, the rear. Gunwales (pronounced "gunnels") form the top of the boat's sides. They too can be made from a number of materials. Thwarts are the supports that extend from one side of the boat to the other. And, naturally, the canoe has seats of some kind.

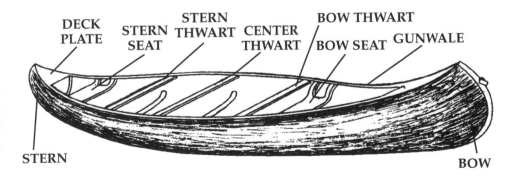

STERN

DECK PLATE STERN SEAT STERN THWART CENTER THWART BOW THWART BOW SEAT GUNWALE

BOW

We'll discuss this interesting world of design and materials in some detail in a moment, but it's important to first note one important, encompassing rule: All designs and materials are a compromise of sorts. There is no such thing as the ideal canoe, only the ideal canoe for your particular needs. You will of course need to identify those needs—by deciding what type of canoeing you'll be doing most of the time—before you make that final, glorious decision of which boat to buy.

CHOOSING A CANOE

Canoe designs have changed dramatically in recent years. Far from the days of "all purpose" canoes, manufacturers are now producing a variety of specialized equipment in amazing combinations of shapes, sizes, and materials—and, of course, with varying price tags.

The first step in purchasing a canoe is to identify your needs. Do you want a racing canoe? One to take touring for a week in the wilderness? One to tackle whitewater? How often will you use it? How much are you willing to spend? After you've considered these and other questions, the next step is to study the differences among the myriad choices.

All canoes are a compromise between speed, maneuverability, and stability.

Speed. A long, thin canoe will inevitably travel faster than a short, wide one will. Having a keel or V-shaped bottom that extends the length of the boat will help it run straighter. Then all of your energy can be directed toward making the boat go fast.

Maneuverability. A short, wide boat will generally be more maneuverable than a long, skinny one. As a result, a fast and maneuverable boat is something of a contradiction in terms.

Stability. A wide design will usually be more stable than a narrow one. Also, a flat-bottomed boat, or one with a shallow V-shaped bottom, will at first seem more stable than a rounded U-shaped hull. So, if you want initial stability, you can't have speed.

SOLO OR TANDEM

To paddle with a partner or without—it's your choice. Most canoes are designed and equipped for two paddlers, though a growing number are now specifically made for solo paddlers. A few models allow you, with a few adjustments in seats and the like, to convert the boat either way.

BASIC CANOE TYPES

To understand the differences between canoes, let's divide them into four general categories: expedition, recreational, slalom, and marathon. There are, of course, many variations on these basic themes.

- Expedition canoes are designed for extended wilderness trips and all the gear they entail. They are often called touring canoes or trippers. These canoes are very stable and have good carrying capacity.
- Recreational canoes are designed for easy river trips and other casual flatwater use. They are easier to turn than expedition canoes, but do not "track" (travel in a straight line) as well.
- Slalom canoes, which are designed to negotiate whitewater, offer exceptional maneuverability. These canoes are short, with round bottoms and a high degree of upturn in the ends (called "rocker"). They are not, however, enjoyable on a long trip because they are difficult to paddle in a straight line.
- Marathon canoes are designed to travel quickly through the water, and are often used for racing. They are long and narrow, making them tippy for novice paddlers. Their straight keel makes them track efficiently, but they're difficult to turn.

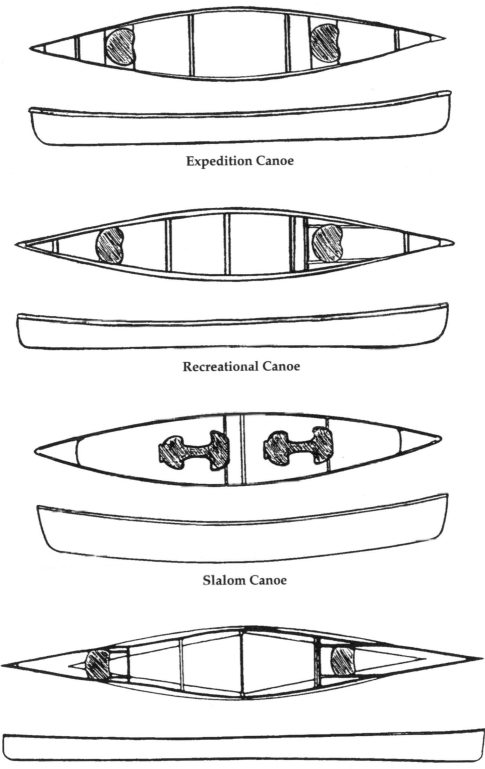

Expedition Canoe

Recreational Canoe

Slalom Canoe

Marathon Canoe

CANOE DESIGN

Canoers, if anything, are an opinionated lot. They know what they like to paddle, and they'll be glad to tell you all about it. A long evening of such conversation will no doubt yield a variety of viewpoints on seemingly esoteric topics like water displacement, stem shape, tumblehome, and rocker, but you will find that the general principles of canoe design are really quite simple.

Hull shape. You'll learn that hulls with flat bottoms, hard chines (sharp, nearly right-angle edges where bottom and sides meet), and tumblehome (curved sides rolling inward at the top) have great initial stability, but almost no secondary stability. In other words, it takes some effort to start them tipping, but once on their way, they're "gone." Conversely, round hulls with soft chines (a gradual curve where bottom and sides meet) and flared sides have much less initial stability, and as a result, they first feel "tippy." But once they start to tip over, they show great secondary stability, and they require some indiscretion from you (or a good boost from wind or waves) to capsize them.

Bow shape. You'll learn that a long, skinny canoe with a bow shaped like a narrow V will be fast. This is because the bow slices through the water rather than bashing into it and piling it up in front of the boat. If instead you make a canoe broad in the beam, and then carry that fullness forward and aft, you have a freighter, not a racer. The canoe may be great for carrying big loads and riding waves, but it will not be quick. Most canoes fall somewhere in between.

Touring canoes. You'll also learn that canoes designed for backcountry travel are asked to do just about everything—carry big loads, endure heavy waves, maintain directional stability, maneuver whitewater, and yet remain relatively easy and fast to paddle. They'll be long enough (seventeen to eighteen-and-a-half feet) to remain fairly narrow even with a beam of thirty-four to thirty-six inches. Entry lines (the taper of the bow) will be slim enough to ease paddling, but then flare at the quarters to improve buoyancy and carrying capacity. There will be some rocker (upward curve in the keel line) to let the boat turn and spin easily, yet not so much that the canoe is impossible to hold on course when crossing a breezy lake.

A knowledgeable canoe dealer with whom you can speak personally may be helpful in making decisions about design. Perhaps better yet is an association with a canoe club where you can meet others who have paddled various models and who will let you try your hand at paddling their boats. There's nothing, after all, like on-the-water testing to determine how you like a particular model. At the very least, you should rent before you buy. It's too big an investment to do otherwise.

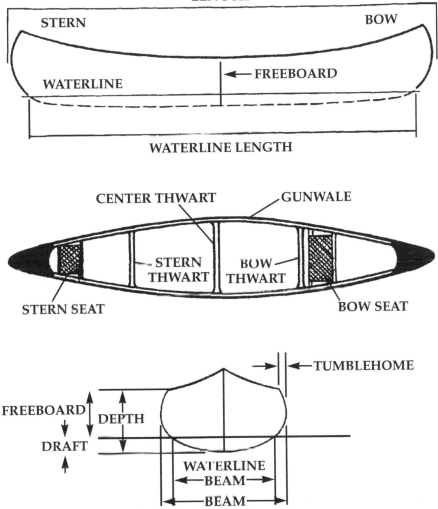

Canoe Design

Length

Canoe length has a tremendous effect on the tracking, maneuverability, and stability of a canoe. Longer canoes have a number of advantages: They are usually easier to paddle, more stable with the same amount of weight, and capable of carrying heavier loads with less loss of performance. They also track better, move faster, and glide farther with each stroke, allowing greater efficiency with less effort. These attributes are especially important on lakes or other calm water, where hairpin turns are not involved.

With a shorter canoe, say fifteen feet, you have to exert more energy to paddle it forward than you would with a longer model. This is why the sixteen- and seventeen-foot lengths are the most popular. The difference between carrying (portaging) a fifteen-foot canoe and a seventeen-foot canoe isn't that great. The weight and price of a particular model are governed more by its materials than by its size.

A longer canoe will also negotiate the waves of a river or wind-tossed lake more smoothly than a short one will. A fifteen-footer will move off center after each oncoming wave, which leaves you fighting to keep on course. Add a foot more length and you suddenly gain stability and a much better ride. Increase the length to eighteen or eighteen-and-a-half feet, and the craft becomes completely manageable, rising and falling gently with the waves.

Long canoes may be more manageable than short ones, but they don't always run drier. If the distance between waves is shorter than the canoe's length, the canoe may plow into the waves and take on significant amounts of water. Under these conditions, a shorter canoe—one that fits between the waves—will be drier, though it might make for a rougher ride.

Shorter canoes are no doubt lighter, less expensive, less cumbersome, and easier to transport. But the most important virtue of a short canoe is quicker turns. A short hull is also preferable for small people or children, and for paddling on narrow streams.

Width

The width of a canoe is typically measured at two points: the beam and the waterline. The beam width is the widest distance between the gunwales or the widest point at the tumblehome. The waterline width is the width of a boat where it rests in the water.

The primary function of width is stability. Wider boats are usually more stable, and are often recommended for fishing and beginners. But handling is sacrificed for that extra width, and the canoe does not work as well in current. A narrower boat has increased efficiency because it brings the paddler's forward strokes closer to the centerline of the canoe.

Additional width adds to carrying capacity (though not as much as length does), but canoes that are too wide require greater effort to paddle, because their hulls push more water.

Depth

The depth of a canoe is measured at the centerline from the gunwale down to the floor of the canoe. A taller boat means more carrying capacity (which is vital in an expedition canoe), and the boat will deflect spray and waves better. But it may also make the boat more vulnerable to the wind. Shallower depth minimizes wind resistance, but increases the probability of shipping water into the boat.

Draft is measured from the waterline to the bottom of the canoe at its deepest point.

Freeboard is measured from the waterline to the top of the gunwale at the center of the canoe. A canoe loaded for a wilderness trip should have at least six inches of freeboard.

Trim is the balance of freeboard from bow to stern and from side to side. Trim can be improved by shifting gear or your position in the boat so that the bow rides slightly higher than the stern. This prevents the bow from plowing through the water.

Symmetry

A canoe's symmetry is the overall shape of the boat from front to back. Some boats are symmetrical, which means that the front half and the back half of the canoe have the same shape; others are asymmetrical, which means the two halves are shaped differently.

Symmetry affects the efficiency of the boat moving through water and its ability to turn. Symmetrical boats are better for quick maneuvering, as in negotiating small streams or whitewater. Asymmetrical boats usually have a lengthened and streamlined bow for more efficient and faster passage through the water. Directional control is increased, but turning ability is decreased.

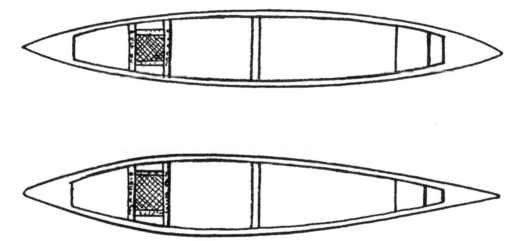

Note the overall difference between symmetrical (above) and asymmetrical (below) canoe design. The symmetrical design is the most common.

Taper

The taper, or entry lines, of a canoe's bow and stern (as viewed from above) is usually described as either full or pointed. A whitewater boat has full ends to give the bow extra volume, so that it can ride over a wave that would otherwise bury it. A fast cruiser, on the other hand, has a very fine, thin bow to knife through the water more easily.

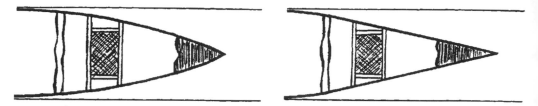

Taper

Rocker

The upturn of the canoe from one end to the other (as viewed from the side of the canoe) is known as rocker. Canoes with a lot of rocker pivot easier because the ends of the canoe sit high in the water and offer little resistance. But these boats do not track (maintain a straight course) well. Canoes with little rocker go straight because the boat resists the turning forces of paddling strokes. These boats do not turn easily because the entire hull sits in the water.

Canoes with a lot of rocker are great for slalom racing or navigating tight streams or tricky whitewater. By contrast, a marathon racing canoe would have no rocker at all, because its goal is straight-ahead speed. Most canoes are a compromise between these two extremes.

SHARP ROCKER

MEDIUM ROCKER

STRAIGHT KEEL LINE

Rocker

Bottom Shapes

The bottom of a canoe (as viewed from its end) ranges from flat-bottomed to V-shaped. Flat-bottomed canoes seem very stable at first. More rounded hulls (those with an arch or shallow V-shape) are initially less stable than flat bottoms, but they have greater secondary stability (and are more forgiving) when the boat is leaned. The more pronounced the V-shape, the better the boat's directional ability, but the worse its stability.

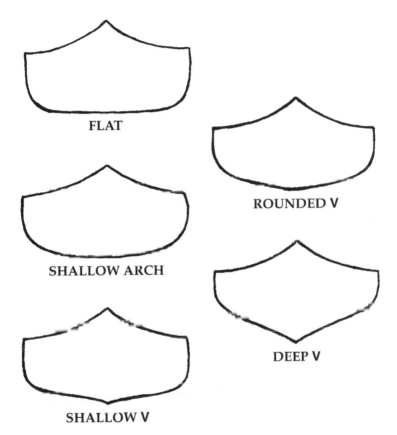

FLAT

ROUNDED V

SHALLOW ARCH

DEEP V

SHALLOW V

Bottom Shapes

Keels

Some canoes, especially those designed for big, windy lakes, have a ridge, known as a keel, running along the bottom from one end to the other. A keel makes the boat track (in a straight line) better, and it reduces slipping from side to side. The advantage of a pronounced keel, however, is largely restricted to lakes, because the keel tends to get caught on the rocks of a river.

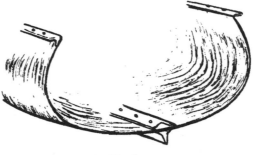

Keels

Chines

The transition between the bottom of the canoe and its sides is called the chine. An abrupt, nearly right-angle transition is called a hard chine, and a smoother, more rounded one is a soft chine. Hard chines have great initial stability, but almost no secondary stability. Soft chines have less initial stability, but great secondary stability.

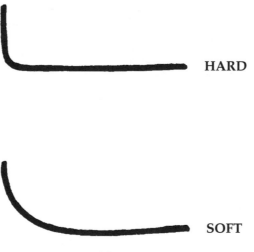

HARD

SOFT

Chines

Flare and Tumblehome

A canoe's sides are described as having flare (leaning outward) or tumblehome (leaning inward), and some canoes, of course, have straight sides. Flare at the top of a canoe helps deflect waves and resist capsizing, which is important for a whitewater canoe. Flare, however, does force you to reach further out of the canoe when paddling, which can be awkward for beginners.

Tumblehome allows the top of the boat to be narrower and therefore easier to paddle. But a canoe with a lot of tumblehome quickly loses stability when it is leaned.

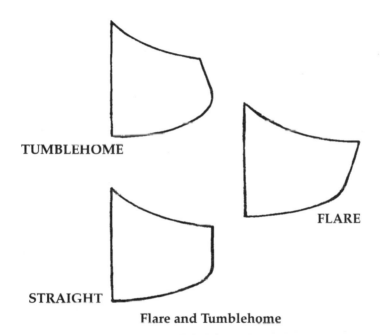

TUMBLEHOME

FLARE

STRAIGHT

Flare and Tumblehome

Stem Shape

The profile of the bow or stern as seen from the side is called the stem. This affects how the boat slices through the water and the amount of water taken into the boat.

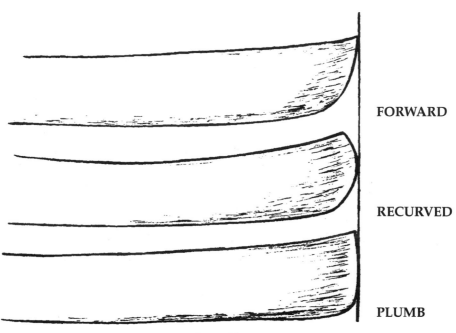

FORWARD

RECURVED

PLUMB

Stem Shape

Weight

A canoe's weight is largely a function of its materials (discussed in detail below). Naturally, the lighter the boat, the easier it is to maneuver. But weight is often sacrificed for the sake of durability.

Carrying Capacity

The most important variable affecting length is the amount of gear you intend to carry. So you'll first need to sit down and figure out how much gear you will have on a typical trip. Most touring canoers find that a high-volume, seventeen- to eighteen-foot boat is the best choice for all-around tandem use. Shorter boats offer certain advantages in handling and control, but they're frequently too small to accommodate all the camping gear you'd like to take.

Touring Considerations

The touring canoe, or "tripper," is incredibly practical for hauling loads that would sink lesser craft. Very few boats of such slender profile can accommodate one's camping gear for a week, or more, on a journey piercing deep into the backcountry. Not made for speed or whitewater, the touring canoe will easily accept your tent, sleeping bags, clothes, food, kitchen utensils, and all the other luxuries that backpackers can only dream about. But not all touring canoes are alike, and inevitably, a friendly debate ensues about which is best. So, in simple terms, what makes for a good touring canoe? Experienced canoers agree on a few basic principles:

- A length of seventeen feet is considered the absolute minimum, and many canoers prefer longer eighteen- or eighteen-and-a-half-foot models.
- The canoe should have substantial depth and volume. Larger canoes not only allow for bigger loads, but also provide a greater margin of safety in rough water.
- Most importantly, you need a good, strong boat for touring. Then, the lighter the boat, the better.
- The canoe must be trustworthy and forgiving on all types of water. A reputable manufacturer is the best assurance of a well-made craft.
- The major concern is safety. The backcountry is no place to experiment with specialized canoes that offer a slight advantage in performance at the expense of strength and predictability.

Canoe Interiors

Any canoe can be customized to suit your individual needs (see the section in chapter 2 on customizing your canoe). Most canoes arrive from the factory in fairly spartan condition, but they at least contain the following:

Gunwales. The rails around the top edges of the canoe should be sturdy, as they take a lot of abuse. Many canoers prefer wood gunwales for their feel and good looks. Wood, however, requires special care. Less attractive aluminum and vinyl gunwales are tough and don't require as much upkeep.

Seats. Seats can be made of plastic, fiberglass, metal, nylon webbing, woven cane, or wood. The type and placement of seats affect not only comfort, but also the strength and stability of the boat. Seats should be low enough to keep the paddler's center of gravity low without inconvenience, and should allow kneeling when desired.

Thwarts. Made from wood or aluminum, the supports that extend from one side of the boat to the other should be sturdy.

Flotation. Some canoes have sealed compartments to keep the canoe afloat even when full of water. Whitewater paddlers usually add more flotation for safety.

CANOE MATERIALS

The materials from which canoes are built are many, and the choices can be intimidating. A canoe designer looks for a material that balances three elements—weight, strength, and cost—in a way that matches a clear vision of how the boat should perform.

Let's start with weight. The lighter the boat, the less water it has to displace as it moves. Naturally, this makes the boat easier to paddle. Weight, however, is often reduced at the expense of durability. With exotic materials, designers can produce a hull that is exceptionally strong and light, but the cost will be high. Strong hulls can be made from less expensive materials, but this usually means a heavier boat. If the canoe is designed for river use, where the current does most of the work and the longest portage is from the car to the put-in, the extra weight may be acceptable. But if you're dealing with lakes or frequent portages, a lighter canoe makes sense.

One way designers balance weight, strength, and cost is to reinforce only those parts that receive the most stress. The ends and bottom of a hull take the most abuse from impact and abrasion, so additional material is placed there. The key is to decide how much (and where) the material is needed to make the hull stiff enough to resist bending, yet flexible enough to distribute stress.

Sometimes a designer has only one logical choice of material for a given design, whereas other models can be offered in two or three different materials. Don't let a certain material keep you from considering a particular canoe, and don't buy a more expensive material than you need. Choose the balance of weight, strength, and cost that matches your idea of what you want your boat to do. Remember: You're buying a boat, not a material.

Most boats manufactured today are made of either plastic, composite, aluminum, or wood. Here's a brief introduction to each.

Plastics

Not all plastics are created alike, and there are considerable differences between them in terms of strength, weight, performance, and maintenance. The two major types of plastics used in the manufacture of canoes are Royalex and molded polyethylene.

Royalex. This plastic consists of a foam core sandwiched between sheets of ABS (acrylonitrile butadiene styrene) with layers of vinyl on top. It is extremely tough—an obvious choice for whitewater and general recreation canoes where durability is important. Royalex requires little maintenance, is relatively easy to repair (though rarely needs it), and is moderately priced. For all these reasons, it's one of the most popular materials.

Molded polyethylene. Polyethylene is inexpensive, durable, slips easily over rocks, and can be molded into complex shapes. There are two common types: linear and cross-linked. Strands of linear polyethylene are very long, whereas cross-linked strands are shorter and chemically bonded to one another. Linear is easier to recycle; cross-linked is stiffer.

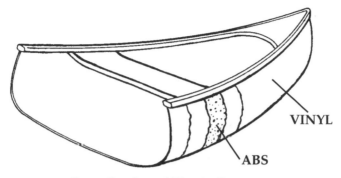

Cross Section of Plastic Canoe

Composites

Composite canoes are made by fitting layers of cloth into a mold and adding resin to create a stiff, tough shell. The most common fabrics are fiberglass and the more durable Kevlar, but composites also include materials like graphite.

A good fiberglass boat can be very tough, though sometimes not durable enough for repeated whitewater use. One type is made of chopped glass fibers mixed with resin and sprayed into a mold, gradually building up the hull. These boats are usually less expensive than those made of fiberglass cloth; they can be durable, but quality varies. A Kevlar boat usually weighs about 25 percent less than its fiberglass counterpart, yet with added strength. Fiberglass and Kevlar can also be combined in a variety of configurations.

All composite materials allow builders to create complex shapes with sharp, efficient lines. The sophistication of these materials is reflected in their high prices. Most composite hulls have an outer layer of gel-coat resin, which protects the fabric from sunlight and abrasion and gives the hull its color and shine. Gel coat, however, can add up to ten pounds to the boat.

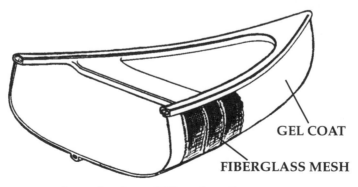

Cross Section of Fiberglass Canoe

Aluminum

The aluminum canoe arose from World War II technology and effectively ended the wood-and-canvas era. Aluminum offered lighter weight, lower cost, no maintenance, and remarkable durability. There are drawbacks, however. Aluminum sticks when scraping over rocks, radiates heat and cold, transmits noise, and lacks aesthetics. With the new plastics and composites now available, aluminum has lost much of its appeal.

Aluminum hulls are made by stretching two metal sheets over a mold, then joining them with rivets along the keel and ends. End caps, thwarts, seats, and gunwales are riveted into place, and then aluminum ribs are spot-welded to stiffen the hull.

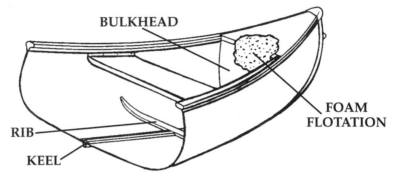

Cross Section of Aluminum Canoe

Wood and Canvas

The wood-and-canvas builder steams the ribs of the canoe to make them flexible and sets them into place over a metal form. Cedar planking is then attached to the ribs with copper nails. Canvas is stretched over the hull and covered with filler to provide a smooth surface. The outside of the hull receives several coats of paint for a watertight finish, the remaining trim is added, and the wood is varnished. The finished boats are beautiful to behold, but expensive. They also require frequent maintenance to keep them in their original condition.

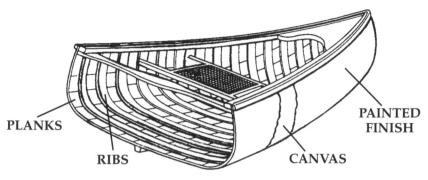

PLANKS

RIBS

CANVAS

PAINTED FINISH

Cross Section of Wood-and-Canvas Canoe

All Wood

These canoes either are made like those of wood and canvas (but without the canvas) or have long, thin planks of wood glued together (the boats are called "strippers") and the hull covered inside and out with fiberglass cloth and resin. Strippers can be molded into highly complex shapes and may be very lightweight. Wooden boats are attractive, but they are expensive and less durable than those made of plastics or composites.

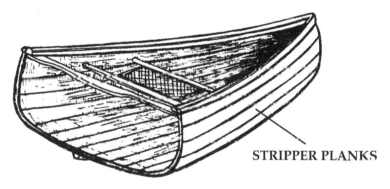

STRIPPER PLANKS

Cross Section of All-Wood Canoe

Other Materials

A number of other materials are available for the manufacture of folding and inflatable canoes.

Folding canoes. Folding craft have a fabric skin of coated nylon or canvas stretched over a wood or aluminum frame. Folding kayaks have been around since the turn of the century, and the longevity of the concept is a testament to their durability. Disassembled, a folding boat fits into two or three duffels that can be checked as luggage or stored in a closet. These

19

boats are slightly less responsive than hardshell canoes, and they can be very expensive.

Inflatable canoes. Serious paddlers used to laugh at these boats. But in recent years inflatable canoes and kayaks have become increasingly sophisticated, and they now offer appealing designs and bombproof materials. The big advantage of inflatables, of course, is their compactness and portability. These boats perform best on whitewater and rivers with current. Newer models are more rigid than ever but still require more effort to paddle on flatwater than a hardshell boat does.

2

Accessories

You have a canoe—now you need to accessorize it. Many canoers customize their craft to make them more comfortable and better suited for whitewater. You'll need to acquire the standard paddling gear: a paddle and a life jacket. You'll also want to buy the right clothing; nothing will be more crucial to your comfort on the water.

CUSTOMIZING YOUR CANOE
Most canoers install custom features like kneepads and painters (short ropes attached to the ends of the canoe). Those who plan to carry (portage) their canoe should consider some type of carrying yoke. Boaters who run whitewater will want to add flotation for safety, and perhaps thigh straps (or even a special kneeling saddle) for better control.

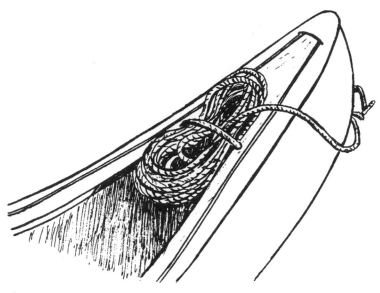

Painter

Painters

The short ropes attached to the bow and stern of the canoe are called painters (apparently an old nautical term). They are useful to tie down a canoe during transport, tie it up at a dock or tree, tow another canoe, or walk the canoe around rapids.

Painters made of three-eighths-inch, bright yellow polypropylene work well because they float and are easy to see in the water. For general recreational paddling, ten- to twelve-foot painters are usually sufficient. On trips where lining (guiding the canoe down rapids with ropes) is a possibility, it may be better to use longer ones (say, twenty to twenty-five feet), or else bring extra line for that purpose.

Some canoes, particularly the plastic models, have places to attach the painters on the bow and stern decks.

Kneepads and Toe Blocks

For comfort while kneeling, many paddlers glue closed-cell foam kneepads on the bottom of the boat. To make your position in the boat even more stable, you can add toe blocks to the bottom of the canoe to keep your feet secure when kneeling.

Thigh Straps

Thigh straps made from nylon webbing are favored by whitewater boaters desiring stability, because thigh straps allow you to paddle with more precision. These straps are inexpensive and are easily folded out of the way when you no longer need them or if the canoe should overturn.

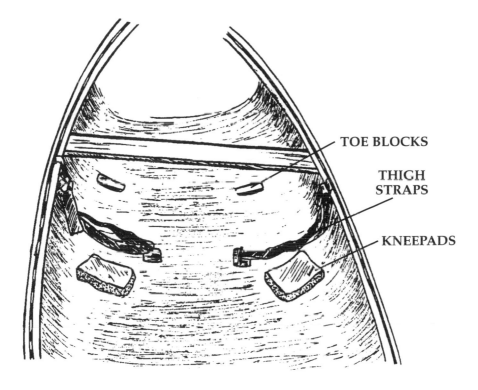

TOE BLOCKS

THIGH
STRAPS

KNEEPADS

Kneeling Saddles

The plastic, customized kneeling saddle is the ultimate in providing a secure position for the paddler. Consider it an elaborate thigh strap that literally allows the boat to move with you, providing the ultimate in control.

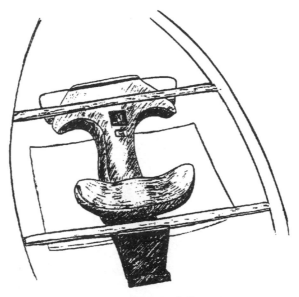

Kneeling Saddle

Flotation

If you are paddling whitewater or large bodies of water, you may want to add additional flotation. The most inexpensive flotation is an inner tube pushed under the center thwart and inflated. Customized flotation—large vinyl air bags or foam blocks—can be purchased for the midsection and ends of the canoe. Whatever flotation you use, be sure to secure it well to avoid losing it.

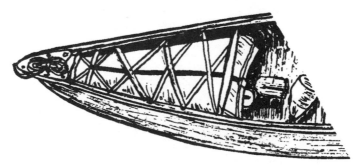

Flotation

Carrying Yokes

If you plan to portage your canoe, you should consider carrying yokes. A good yoke will distribute the weight of your canoe evenly on your shoulders. There are two types of yokes. One, made of hardwood curved to fit your shoulders, replaces the center thwart. Another bolts over the existing center thwart and comes with foam pads for your shoulders. Some boaters use paddles lashed across the thwarts; these are less comfortable but are better than nothing.

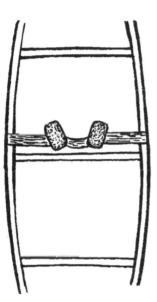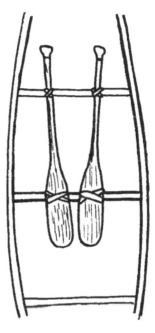

Carrying Yokes

Thwart Bags

Another useful accessory, the thwart bag, simply attaches underneath the thwart or seat to provide easy access to those things needed during the day—sunglasses, lip balm, suntan lotion, mosquito repellent, and so forth.

Thwart Bag

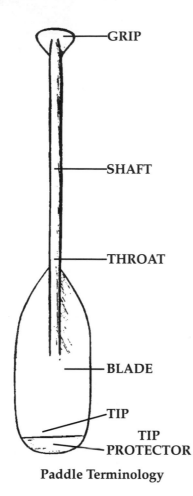

GRIP

SHAFT

THROAT

BLADE

TIP

TIP
PROTECTOR

Paddle Terminology

PADDLES

A good touring paddle should be light, strong, and well balanced. The choice of design, material, and size is not as easy as it would first appear. The decision is an important one: After paddling hundreds, even thousands, of strokes a day, the wrong choice will be very evident to your arm and back muscles.

Design

Designs of canoe paddles can be almost as varied as the designs of canoes, and the final decision of which to buy should depend on the type of canoeing you plan to do and personal preference.

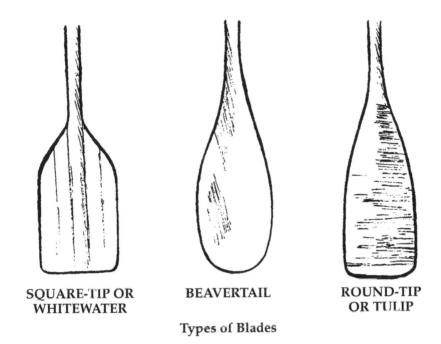

SQUARE-TIP OR WHITEWATER **BEAVERTAIL** **ROUND-TIP OR TULIP**

Types of Blades

Blades. The most basic blade shape is rectangular, but the trend in recent years has been toward smaller, faster blades with a so-called tulip shape. Also popular is the long, narrow beavertail design, which is excellent for subtle steering maneuvers.

Large blades work on the theory that the more water you move, the more power you have. But most canoers now believe that a strong stroke is a matter of blade control, not size. A slightly smaller blade is preferable if you anticipate a lot of flatwater or wind. A blade with a rounded edge will enter the water more crisply.

T-SHAPED **PEAR-SHAPED**

Types of Grips

Grips. The grip of a paddle is important because it's where most of the control comes from. Many paddlers prefer a T-shaped grip because it provides greater control (especially in whitewater), but the pear-shaped grip is favored by others for its comfort.

Handles. The two choices here are round and oval, and boaters seem to disagree on which is the most comfortable.

Bent-Shaft Paddles. A bent-shaft paddle, where the blade is set at an angle of five to fifteen degrees to the shaft, allows for a very efficient stroke. This is because the blade stays vertical until almost the end of the stroke. Bent-shaft paddles are great for propulsion and provide better control than straight-shaft models. But the bent-shaft uses the same face for all paddling strokes, so reversing the blade (as in certain maneuvers, like a low brace) is awkward.

Bent-Shaft Paddle

Materials

Paddles are made of various materials, and each has a different feel, weight, and durability. A lively debate is ongoing among canoers about which is the most desirable.

Wood. Most wood paddles are made from strips of wood glued or laminated together. Sitka spruce, western red cedar, and ash are common materials. Many of the better models are covered with a protective layer of fiberglass, and others are finished with varnish. Tips are often reinforced with hardwood or fiberglass, or capped with metal or plastic. Wood, while beautiful, is expensive and requires frequent care. Wooden paddles, even those from the same manufacturer, may vary considerably in weight, balance, and beauty. But many paddlers feel that wood's pleasing flexibility can't be duplicated in a synthetic material.

Wood Paddle

Synthetics. Paddles made of fabrics such as Kevlar, graphite, and carbon fiber are light and strong, but they're expensive. Fiberglass occupies the middle ground in price, weight, and durability. Some surprisingly good, yet inexpensive, paddles are made with fiberglass blades and aluminum shafts. Other paddles are made out of molded ABS plastic; these are durable and inexpensive, but heavy. The weight of a paddle is important, and how it's distributed makes a big difference in the "feel" of the paddle. Some paddlers prefer a thick blade because it seems to "stick" to the water. Other boaters choose a thin blade because it "seems" faster.

Plastic-and-Aluminum Paddle

Size
Beware of misinformation about the correct paddle length. Some recommend a paddle that extends to your chin when standing, but in many cases this is far too long. Most paddles, if placed upright, should extend to somewhere between your chest and shoulders. The stern paddler might need an inch or two more length than the bow paddler, who will find a shorter paddle easier to swing from side to side.

The paddle should be long enough to allow good leverage, yet short enough to be moved quickly. The shorter the paddle, the more you have to compensate with your body to reach. Skill level makes a difference: An experienced paddler can get good leverage with a shorter paddle.

When the blade is completely submerged, the top of the handle should be at chin or eye level. To find the right length on dry land, sit or kneel on a chair to simulate the same height that you would sit or kneel in a canoe. Now hold the paddle in front of you. When the throat of the shaft is level with the seat of the chair, you should be looking at or slightly over the handle. This is approximately the correct shaft length, although you may vary it a few inches either way to accommodate your individual style. To that you must add the length of the blade.

For most people, length will range from fifty-six to fifty-nine inches, with a blade seven-and-a-half to eight inches wide and eighteen to twenty inches long. If you want a bent-shaft paddle, you might start with a fifty-two-inch paddle. The choice is a subjective one, so try various lengths before you buy.

LIFE JACKETS

Few pieces of boating gear have progressed more in comfort and safety than the life jacket. The "personal flotation device," or PFD, as they are called by the Coast Guard, can generally be described by their type.

For safety, you'll need a Type III or Type V PFD. Type III PFDs, usually shorter and with flotation "ribs" rather than "slabs," are designed for canoers and kayakers who require more freedom of motion than Type V PFDs allow. The Type V category covers special designs for whitewater, generally with commercial raft passengers in mind. These jackets offer greater flotation and safety than the Type III, but tend to be bulkier and more restrictive. (Incidentally, Type I is the bulky, orange "Mae West" jacket filled with kapok; Type II is the horse-collar version, which is inadequate for river use; and Type IV is a buoyant seat cushion, unsuitable for just about everything.)

Life Jacket

When choosing a PFD, favor safety over comfort. PFDs designed for hardshell kayakers often have extra flotation in the area below the waist, and these can be flipped up for comfort. The amount of flotation you require in a life jacket depends primarily on your body's own flotation, your experience, and the kind of whitewater you'll be tackling.

For easy rivers, a "shortie" Type III offers a good measure of safety and unrestricted motion. In whitewater, a Type V or a high-flotation version of a Type III is better. There should be sufficient buckles and straps to secure the jacket firmly around your body. You'll want to wear the PFD snugly to keep it from riding up over your head, so make certain your jacket fits well.

Always fasten all buckles, zippers, and waist-ties when you put the life jacket on. Never wear the PFD loose or open in the front, and pull the side straps down snug. This is also important to avoid entangling yourself should the boat overturn. Make a habit, too, of securing your life jacket when you take it off, so the wind doesn't blow it away.

A good PFD will give you years of protection if treated properly. Don't use your life jacket as a seat cushion. After each trip, hang the jacket to maintain its shape and prevent it from getting mildew. Clean it often, using a mild soap so as not to harm the interior foam.

CLOTHING

Veteran river runners agree when it comes to clothing: Buy the best and cut corners somewhere else. A boater's enjoyment is too dependent on climate and water temperatures to do otherwise. With new synthetic fabrics and insulation incorporated into clothing designed just for boaters, there's no reason to be uncomfortable.

Cold Weather

The most versatile way to stay warm in cold weather involves layering, with clothing added or removed to regulate the body's heat. Layering works well if there are periods of exertion (layers removed) followed by periods of rest (layers added)—which is the usual routine on canoe trips. The standard line of advice is to start with an inner layer of long underwear, add additional layers of insulation as needed, and then top it off with a waterproof shell.

Synthetics. If there's the slightest chance you'll get wet (and there usually is), the obvious advantage of synthetic fabrics is their ability to dry quickly, and pile and fleece work well in this regard. They are also extremely rugged and require little care. How well these materials keep you warm is largely dependent on their thickness, and so their only drawback is their bulk: They don't compress well for packing.

Underwear. If weather or water turns really cold, you'll need long underwear. Polypropylene is popular because it keeps moisture off the skin. Polyester fabrics (under trade names like Capilene) have been introduced that pill less and remain softer than polypropylene. Even though polypropylene and polyester don't offer much insulation, the body is warmer when it's dry. Different thicknesses are now available for diverse situations.

In even colder weather, you can add additional layers of thinner synthetic fabrics, or you can use a thicker synthetic fill. For use on the water, goose or duck down is useless, because it takes days to dry. Wool is a good insulator when wet, though it becomes heavy and stretches; it's also slow to dry. With the new synthetics, wool has lost most of its appeal.

Paddling Jacket

Shell. Regardless of inner layers, a waterproof outer layer—a raincoat and pants, a paddling jacket, or a drysuit—is necessary to keep the inner layers dry and to prevent heat loss. According to the experts, wool is hardly warmer than cotton unless you cover it with a shell.

31

Kayakers, recognizing the advantages of a waterproof shell, developed the paddling jacket with its tight-fitting closures. The logical extension is a pair of paddling pants, complete with neoprene ankle cuffs or drysuit seals.

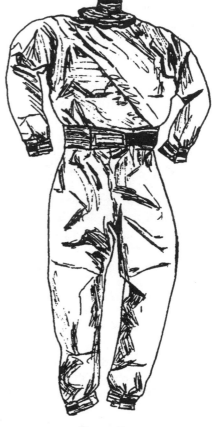

Drysuit

Wetsuit

Wetsuits. A neoprene wetsuit is commonly used in frigid conditions because the thin layer of water trapped underneath is warmed by the body's heat and acts as insulation.

Drysuits. A drysuit, with its loose body and tight-fitting vinyl seals at neck, wrist, and ankles, allows insulation to be worn underneath. Many boaters find drysuits more comfortable than wetsuits, but drysuits are also more expensive and difficult to maintain than wetsuits.

Extremities. Don't forget the extremities—head, hands, feet. The head is a critical area of heat loss, since over half the body's heat can be lost there. Any type of hat will help, but in cold weather, a close-fitting wool or synthetic cap provides more warmth. Synthetic gloves will retain warmth when wet, but neoprene ones are warmer (though they can be tiring to use, due to the material's tendency to spring back to its original shape).

Wetsuit boots (with hard soles) and wet-suit socks (without) are the best protection against cold water sloshing around the bottom of the boat. (A thin polypropylene liner-sock underneath will keep your feet drier, and therefore warmer.) Wetsuit boots have become increasingly sophisticated with zippers, lace-up tops, padded insoles, and traction soles.

Wetsuit Boots

Warm Weather

In warm weather, you can wear just about anything and get away with it. Quick-drying fabrics are still more comfortable (which rules out denim jeans), and clothing made just for river runners is available. Ubiquitous footwear among canoers is the river sandal.

Sandals

3

Basic Strokes

It's a beautiful sight. Paddles dipping up and down, in and out of the water, like a bird's wings, to steer the canoe through rocky stretches of the river's rapids or across a wide expanse of lake. Behind these graceful motions are canoers working hard with the tools of their trade.

Almost anyone with average strength and coordination can become proficient in the basic paddle strokes after a few hours of practice. Beginning on flatwater is easiest. To gain confidence, start on a small lake or in a swimming pool. Then you can take your newly acquired paddling skills to a broad, slow river.

ENTERING THE CANOE

To enter the canoe without capsizing, you need to avoid putting all of your weight on one side of the craft. In a tandem canoe, the stern paddler should steady the canoe while the bow paddler—with one hand on each gunwale—makes his way to the front of the canoe. The stern paddler, holding one hand on each gunwale, puts one foot on the deck forward of the stern seat and shoves away from the bank with the other, climbing into the canoe as it becomes waterborne.

The solo canoer boards much the same way: grasping both gunwales, putting one foot inside the canoe, shoving off, and then getting all the way in as the canoe moves away.

Entering the Canoe

SEATING POSITION

Most of the time you'll be sitting in the canoe. But in high waves and whitewater, it's better to kneel on the deck because this lowers your center of gravity and reduces the chances of capsizing. For the best stability, kneel with your backside against the front of your seat and spread your knees against the sides of the canoe.

There are actually three seating positions in a canoe:
- Kneeling down, with both knees pushed as far apart as is comfortable.
- Kneeling on one knee, allowing you to paddle more powerfully and efficiently. (You should of course kneel on the side you are paddling.)
- Sitting on the seat, which may be the most comfortable position, but is less efficient and gives you the least amount of control.

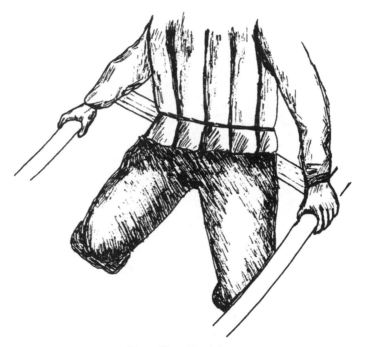

Kneeling Position

When you're sitting in the canoe, it's important to find a comfortable position in which your knees are below the gunwales. If your knees are above the gunwales, you will have to lift your paddle over them.

The bow and stern paddlers should paddle on opposite sides of the canoe to maintain balance and travel in a straight line. Switching sides periodically reduces muscle fatigue, but you should do so in coordination with your partner. It's also a good idea to switch positions between bow and stern, which is best done leap-frog style.

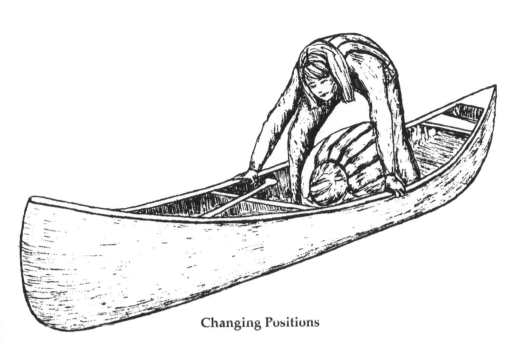

Changing Positions

EXITING THE CANOE

The usual way to exit a canoe is to drive the bow gently into shore so the
bow paddler can step out onto dry land and pull the canoe farther up the
bank. The bow paddler then steadies the canoe while the stern paddler
puts one hand on each gunwale and walks down the canoe to step ashore.

Exiting the Canoe

PADDLING STROKES

Paddling strokes can be divided into three major groups: power strokes, turning strokes, and bracing strokes.

- Power strokes propel the canoe forward or backward.
- Turning (or corrective) strokes move the canoe in a new direction or bring the canoe back on course.
- Bracing strokes provide stability, though they can be used to turn the boat. They are most often used in whitewater.

Strokes are also described as dynamic, when the paddler pulls on the blade, and static, when the paddler plants the blade and holds it, letting the momentum of the boat or the pull of the current complete the stroke.

It's best to learn and practice the strokes in their pure form. With experience, you can combine power and turning strokes into one smooth motion. This chapter discusses the basic power strokes: the forward stroke (along with the corrective J-stroke and C-stroke) and the back stroke. The next chapter discusses the turning strokes—the sweep, the draw, and the pry—and the bracing strokes, the low brace and the high brace.

GRIPPING THE PADDLE

To determine where you should grip the paddle, hold the paddle just over your head. Your grip on the shaft is correct when your elbows form right angles. This is the basic grip, though it will be varied slightly to meet circumstances we'll discuss below.

Holding the Paddle

A LITTLE TERMINOLOGY

Canoeing isn't about technicalities, of course, but a little terminology is helpful to explain the paddling stroke.

Phases of the Stroke

The phases of the stroke are described by the following:
- The catch, or plant, phase is the starting point of a stroke.
- The power, or propulsion, phase is the application of force with the paddle against the water, which causes the canoe to move.
- The recovery phase involves the return of the paddle blade back to the original catch position, which involves feathering the blade above the water or slicing it through the water.

Faces of the Paddle

The sides of the paddle blade used in strokes are described as follows:
- The power face is the side of the paddle that pushes against the water during the forward stroke.
- The backface (or nonpower face) is the opposite side, i.e., the back of the blade. During the back stroke, the backface pushes the water.

POWER FACE ⟶ ◀— NONPOWER FACE

Faces of the Paddle

Pivot Point

The point around which the boat turns is called the pivot point. It is usually near the center of the boat, but the pivot point can change.

One important factor affecting the pivot point is the distribution of weight in the boat. Another factor is the accumulation of external forces. For example, when the boat initially accelerates, the pivot point moves toward the stern, but when the boat moves forward under constant power, the pivot point moves toward the bow. When the paddler shifts his weight to one side of the boat, as in an eddy turn, the pivot point shifts.

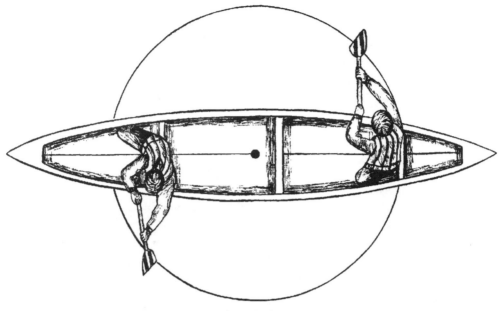

Pivot Point

SOLO VS. TANDEM

In a tandem canoe, the bow paddler provides most of the power and only a small part of the steering. The stern paddler provides less power because he will be putting more effort into steering. Therefore, the more skilled paddler typically takes the stern.

Both solo and tandem strokes will be covered in this book, but we'll start with solo paddling and concentrate on each stroke in its pure form. Tandem strokes are mostly a combination of solo strokes, and those combinations will be covered in the next chapter.

FORWARD STROKE

The forward stroke is the standard power stroke. Because it's so instinctive, many paddlers think it requires little discussion: Just place the paddle in the water and pull. However, there is much more to this stroke than meets the eye, and proper form can make a huge difference in its effect. The key is using the heavier muscles of the torso rather than the arms alone. The forward stroke is made close to the side of the boat, with the paddle shaft moving on a nearly vertical plane to the water.

Catch
- To begin the stroke, extend the lower arm full length and bend the upper arm at the elbow. If you're on the right side of the canoe, thrust your right shoulder forward by rotating your body at the waist. Do not extend the paddle by leaning forward.
- Place the blade close to the boat and dip it almost completely into the water.

Power
- Most of the power of a forward stroke is delivered in the first five to seven inches of the paddle's travel, as the torso unwinds. It makes sense, then, to explode on the stroke; that is, to put everything you have into the first part of the stroke, rather than keeping the pull even. Several short, powerful strokes are better than one long one.
- Keep your right arm straight but not stiff. The left arm stays slightly bent at about eye level.
- Keep the paddle vertical, and keep the power flowing parallel to the boat's centerline.
- The right arm pulls backward until the hand is near the hip. Bringing the paddle back any farther wastes time and power. At this point, both arms are relaxed, with the upper arm dropping down.

Recovery
- This action causes the blade to rise to the surface of the water, and the stroke can now begin again

In executing the forward stroke, only a slight rotation of the body and shoulders should accompany the arm motion. Eliminating unnecessary body motion allows greater smoothness and efficiency. Use the stronger and larger muscles of your back, abdomen, and upper body. Uncoil your body, keep your arms straight, and make your shoulder and stomach muscles do the work.

We'll now take a look at both the side view and the front view of the forward stroke.

Forward Stroke—Side View

Forward Stroke—Front View

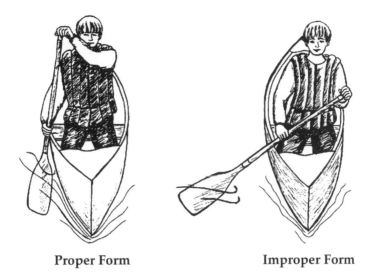

Proper Form   **Improper Form**

Movement of the Canoe

When you execute the forward stroke, you might expect the canoe to move straight ahead. Unfortunately, this is not the case. A canoe tends to turn whenever you make a stroke. A forward stroke on the right side causes the canoe to veer left. A forward stroke on the left side causes the canoe to veer right. This unbalanced situation requires the paddler to propel and steer the boat at the same time.

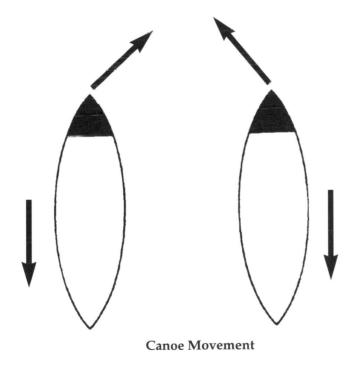

Canoe Movement

THE J-STROKE: A CORRECTIVE FOR TANDEM CANOERS

As we've seen, even if you have a good forward stroke, there's still the problem of unintentional turning of the boat. To keep the boat going in a straight line, the paddler must use some sort of correction stroke.

Solo paddlers have to put in a corrective stroke with almost every power stroke. Tandem paddlers fare better, since the bow and stern paddlers balance each other to some extent. Even so, the stern paddler must frequently make corrective strokes.

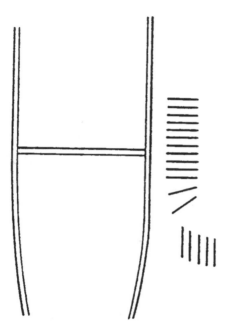

The most elementary corrective stroke used to compensate for this slight deviation is a stern rudder. The rudder, however, creates excessive drag and makes paddling in unison difficult. Using a J-stroke as a corrective stroke will keep the canoe tracking straight without affecting forward speed. The J-stroke allows a quick and subtle correction at the end of the stroke. The J-stroke is basically a forward stroke with a turning stroke added at the end. At the end of each forward stroke, twist your top hand to turn your blade perpendicular to the water. Give a quick outward hook to provide the correcting push-away force.

Path of the Paddle

Proper Grip

J-Stroke

THE C-STROKE:
A CORRECTIVE FOR SOLO
CANOERS

The stern paddler in a tandem canoe uses a J-stroke to keep the canoe on a straight course. In solo paddling, the J-stroke is modified into a stroke more or less resembling the letter C. The paddle is extended forward and slightly out from the gunwale, then brought back in an inward sweep, ending in an outward sweep.

C-Stroke

Paddle Switch Technique

PADDLE SWITCH

When paddling long, skinny touring boats in flatwater, there is another technique for keeping the boat straight: It's called the paddle switch, the sit 'n' switch, or the Minnesota switch. It consists of using forward strokes taken alternately on either side of the boat, using them to balance the boat's tendency to turn.

The solo paddler takes several forward strokes on one side of the boat, then switches hands and puts in several more strokes on the other side, keeping the boat straight under power. Any time lost by switching sides is more than compensated for by not having to use the less efficient corrective strokes. It is often done with a bent-shaft paddle while sitting rather than kneeling (hence the name sit 'n' switch).

Tandem boats use a similar system. Even if the paddlers are stroking on opposite sides, the canoe will drift slightly to one side. Switching sides at the same time, they can correct for this movement. When switching sides, the bow paddler sets the pace for the switch.

BACK STROKE

The back stroke is basically the reverse of the forward stroke. It begins where the forward stroke ends.

The bottom arm pushes down and forward, while the upper arm pulls up and back. At the beginning of the stroke, the body leans somewhat forward, and at the end of the stroke, somewhat backward. This stroke uses the muscles of the abdomen, arms, and shoulders, and to execute it it's necessary to keep a steady, erect posture.

In still water, the back stroke moves the boat upstream. In fast water, it slows the downstream speed of the boat, allowing better visibility of obstacles downstream.

Back Stroke

47

FARBACK STROKE

The farback stroke is an exaggerated version of the back stroke. Its advantage is that it's easier to keep the boat going straight in a reverse direction.

To implement the farback stroke, the paddler rotates her body as far toward the stern as she can. She then reverses her paddle and plants the power face almost vertical behind her. When the stroke is taken, it extends no farther than the paddler's body. The paddler then feathers the blade and begins another stroke.

Farback Stroke

4

Advanced Strokes

Once you've mastered the basic power strokes (especially the forward stroke and its corrective strokes), you're ready to move to the turning strokes: the sweep, the draw, and the pry. Tandem canoers, of course, will have to coordinate these strokes among themselves, and we'll discuss those maneuvers in detail.

After you've perfected these turning strokes, you'll then want to practice the static "support" strokes, called bracing strokes, most notably the low brace and the high brace.

SWEEP STROKES

When making turns, canoers can make good use of the sweep strokes. The sweep is also useful for shallow water and meandering creeks. In a sweep stroke, you use the same basic technique as regular forward and back strokes, except the sweep is an exaggerated arc out and away from the boat. Here you want the paddle to be as far from the pivot point as possible in order to increase the leverage of the stroke. It's this extra reach that gives the stroke more power than a regular forward or back stroke. Best of all, you lose no momentum.

Forward Sweep

The forward sweep, like a forward stroke, will push the bow away from your paddling side—only much more dramatically. Thus, a forward sweep on the right moves the canoe to the left. A forward sweep on the left moves the canoe to the right.

To make a full forward sweep, the blade of the paddle should start as far forward as possible. Plant the blade and rotate your torso, spinning the boat in a circle. Body rotation is essential to the sweep stroke.

Keep your arms straight and the paddle blade well away from the boat. Finish with the paddle behind you and almost touching the stern. It is permissible to lean slightly forward or back, but try to keep good posture during the stroke.

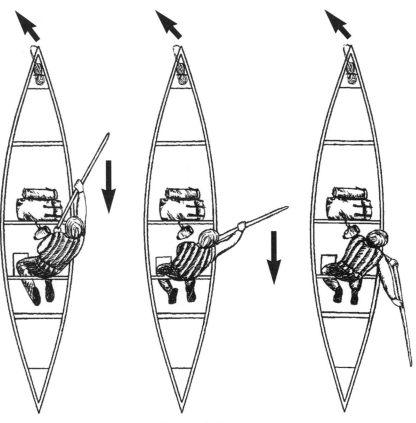

Forward Sweep

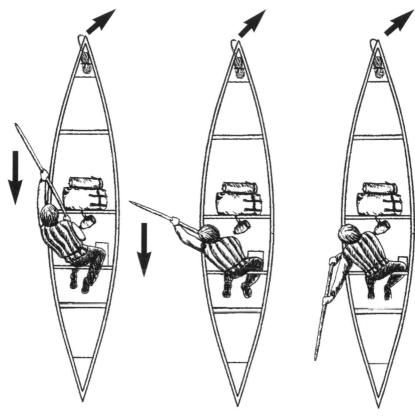

Forward Sweep

Reverse Sweep

The reverse sweep is done the same way as the forward sweep, except the paddle blade starts at the stern of the boat and ends at the bow.

The reverse sweep pushes the stern toward your paddling side, much like a back stroke—only much more dramatically. Thus, a reverse sweep on the right moves the canoe to the right. A reverse sweep on the left moves the canoe to the left.

Start the reverse sweep with your paddle as far back and as close to the stern as possible. Push the water in an arc using the backface of your paddle. The most effective part of the reverse sweep is the first twelve inches closest to the stern.

Avoid the common mistake of confusing a reverse sweep with a back stroke, which kills the speed of the boat. The "half" reverse sweep (starting at the stern and ending at a right angle to the boat) is a common corrective stroke on whitewater, but instead of using a reverse sweep, many paddlers place the paddle behind them and push forward, making a back stroke.

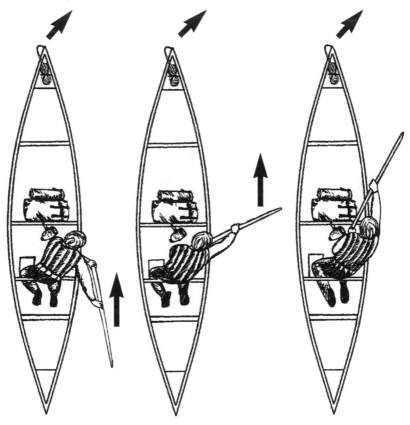

Reverse Sweep

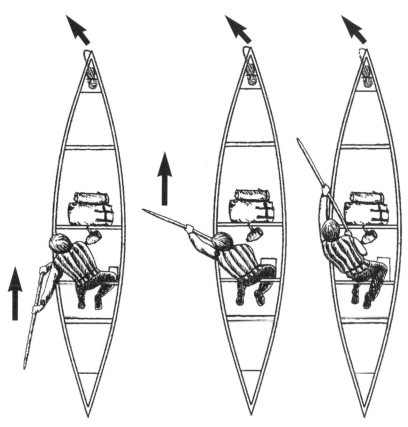

Reverse Sweep

DRAW STROKE

Another very useful turning stroke is the draw stroke. The draw stroke quickly moves the boat sideways toward the paddle. Thus, a draw stroke on the right moves the canoe to the right. A draw stroke on the left moves the canoe to the left.

To execute the draw stroke, reach out as far as possible with the power face of the paddle facing you. Maintain the paddle in a vertical position. Pull (or "draw") your paddle toward the canoe. When your paddle almost reaches the canoe, turn your top hand away and slice the blade of the paddle out of the water. You can then return the paddle to the catch position to begin the stroke again.

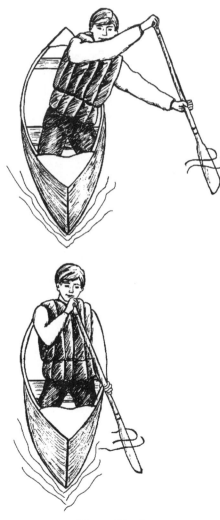

Draw Stroke

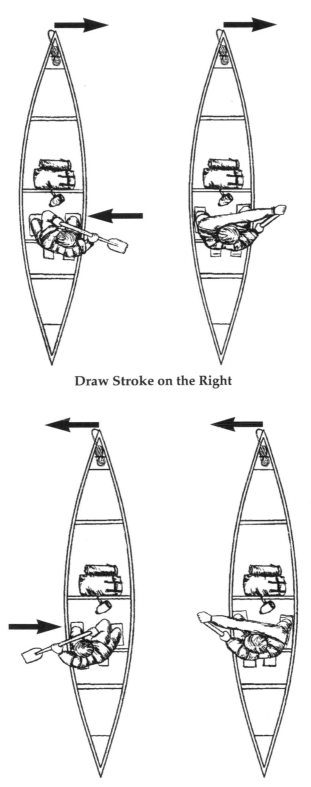

Draw Stroke on the Right

Draw Stroke on the Left

CROSS DRAW

The cross draw is a draw stroke performed by the bow or solo paddler on the side opposite the one on which he has been paddling. As a result, this usually puts the bow paddler in a tandem canoe on the same side as the stern paddler. The cross draw, naturally, pulls the canoe toward the side of the bow or solo paddler. Without changing the position of your hands on the paddle, rotate your upper torso and lift the paddle over and across the bow. Plant the paddle at a forty-five-degree angle to the keel line. Your top hand will be at shoulder level and your lower arm will be extended. The power in the cross draw comes when you use your entire torso, not just your arms, to pull the paddle to the bow, just as you would in a typical draw stroke.

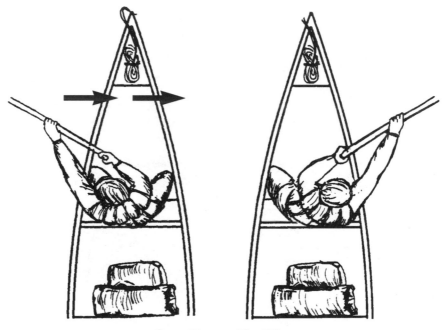

Cross Draw—Top View

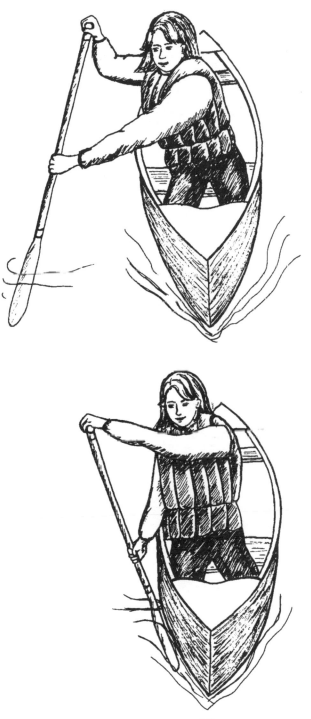

Cross Draw—Front View

PRY STROKE

The opposite of the draw stroke is the pry stroke, which is a sideways push (or "pry") of the paddle away from the canoe. A pry stroke on the right moves the canoe to the left, and a pry stroke on the left moves the canoe to the right.

Start the pry stroke with the paddle shaft near the side of the boat, with the blade underneath the canoe, and with your upper arm over the water. Push with your lower arm while pulling your upper arm toward you. For added power, you can pry the paddle off the gunwale of the canoe. When your paddle is vertical, you should stop the stroke.

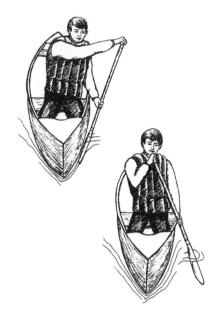

Pry Stroke

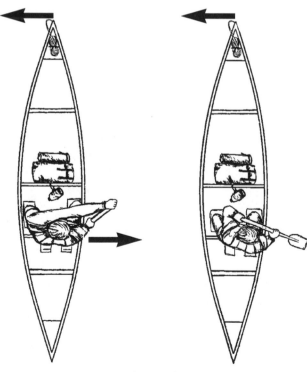

Pry Stroke on the Right

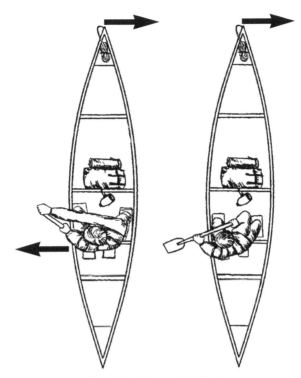

Pry Stroke on the Left

TANDEM STROKES

Now we turn to the seemingly complicated subject of tandem turning strokes—and the art of coordinating those strokes between the bow paddler and the stern paddler. They say there's more than one way to skin a cat, and tandem paddling is no exception. Remember: Most of the turning is done by the stern paddler, though the bow paddler can add significantly to the strength and speed of the turn.

We'll first look at the most common seating situation—the stern paddler on the right side of the canoe and the bow paddler on the left side. Then we'll look at the opposite situation—the stern paddler on the left and the bow paddler on the right. In each instance, we'll show you how to make turns with various combinations of sweep strokes, draw strokes, and pry strokes.

Take heart: Tandem strokes are not as confusing as they first appear, and they will soon become second nature with a little practice between you and your partner.

Four ways to turn a canoe to the left when the stern paddler is on the right.

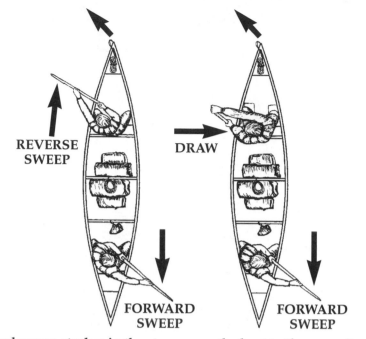

Forward sweep strokes in the stern move the boat to the opposite side, aided by strokes in the bow.

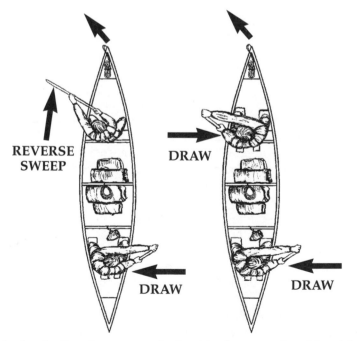

Draw strokes in the stern move the boat to the opposite side, aided by strokes in the bow.

Four ways to turn a canoe to the right when the stern paddler is on the right.

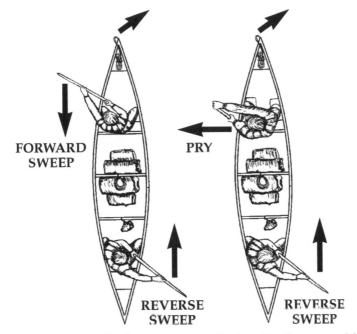

FORWARD
SWEEP

PRY

REVERSE
SWEEP

REVERSE
SWEEP

Reverse sweep strokes in the stern move the boat to the same side, aided by strokes in the bow.

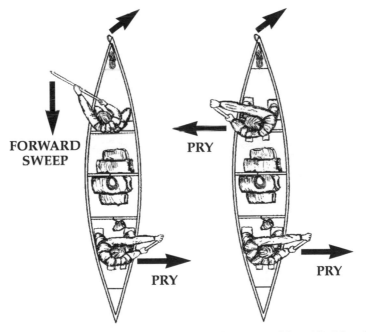

FORWARD
SWEEP

PRY

PRY

PRY

Pry strokes in the stern move the boat to the same side, aided by the strokes in the bow.

Four ways to turn a canoe to the left when the stern paddler is on the left.

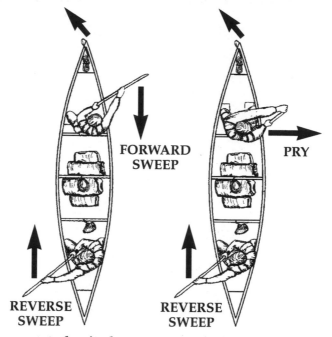

Reverse sweep strokes in the stern move the boat to the same side, aided by strokes in the bow.

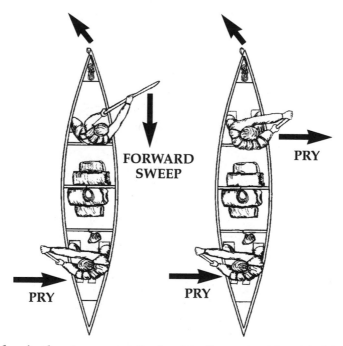

Pry strokes in the stern move the boat to the same side, aided by strokes in the bow.

Four ways to turn a canoe to the right when the stern paddler is on the left.

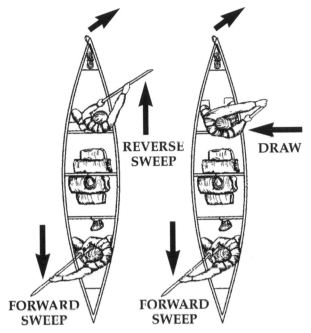

REVERSE SWEEP

DRAW

FORWARD SWEEP

FORWARD SWEEP

Forward sweep stroke in the stern moves the boat to the opposite side, aided by strokes in the bow.

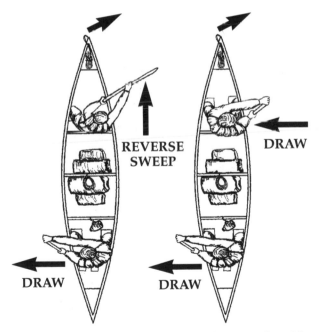

REVERSE SWEEP

DRAW

DRAW

DRAW

Draw strokes in the stern move the boat to the opposite side, aided by strokes in the bow.

Left turn and right turn with cross draw strokes.

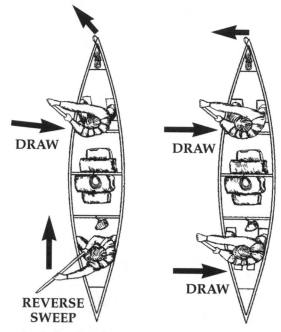

DRAW

DRAW

**REVERSE
SWEEP**

DRAW

Cross draw on the left side of the bow naturally moves the boat to the left, aided by strokes in the stern.

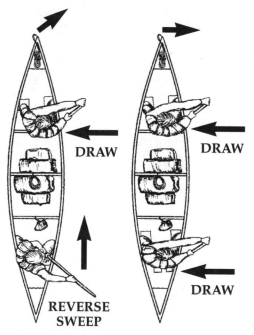

DRAW

DRAW

**REVERSE
SWEEP**

DRAW

Cross draw on the right side of the bow naturally moves the boat to the right, aided by strokes in the stern.

BRACING STROKES

Experienced canoers make good use of bracing strokes, which utilize the paddle as a lever to provide stability by using the force of the water to keep the boat right side up. On a river you must always lean and brace downstream. Leaning upstream will cause you to capsize. There are two forms of brace: a low brace and a high brace.

Low Brace

The low brace is used when the canoe suddenly leans toward the side on which you are paddling. To execute a low brace, you reach out of the canoe with a nearly horizontal paddle. The key to the low brace is a stern thrust of the paddle on the water, which helps push you back to the upright position.

Low Brace

High Brace

High Brace
The high brace is used when the canoe leans away from the side on which you are paddling. It's as if you are grasping onto the water with your paddle to pull yourself into the upright position.

DUFFEK STROKE

The Duffek stroke (named after the famous Czech expatriate paddler, Milo Duffek) allows the paddler to turn the boat by planting the paddle in the water near the bow and letting either the momentum of the boat or the current pull the canoe around the paddle.

The Duffek starts like a draw stroke, except the blade angle is increased so that the power face of the blade faces somewhat away from the boat. The force of the water will feel as if it is pulling the paddle away from the canoe. Hold the Duffek until the boat has turned far enough, and then draw the paddle back to the bow.

Duffek Stroke

5

Reading Currents

They call it reading whitewater—the science that boaters have of evaluating a stretch of rapids to determine the route through the boulders and hydraulics that will provide the least chance of damage to gear, and themselves.

It's a misnomer, really, because reading whitewater isn't quite as much science as art, and as with all fine arts, there is more than one way to do it well. With that said, there are still a few basic principles that allow boaters to better size up those intimidating rapids below.

As a beginning boater, you should of course hone your skills first on lakes and other flatwater. Then you can try your hand at a slow-moving stream that offers little in the way of obstacles. After you're comfortable with that, you can gradually move to slightly more difficult rivers. That way, you never find yourself in a situation you can't handle.

TYPES OF RIVERS
Much can be learned about how a river works by simple observation. Spend time studying moving water and how it is affected by the obstacles it encounters.

Look upstream at a stretch of rapids and notice where rocks are located. Then walk to the head of the rapids and look downstream to see how the rocks appear from a river runner's point of view. Watch other boaters run the rapids, and note where they position their craft.

Every river looks different, yet they all follow the same basic rules. Rivers basically vary according to their volume, their gradient, and their velocity. A river with rapids that alternate with long quiet stretches is known as a pool-and-drop river, as opposed to one that drops steadily over its length. Pool-and-drop rivers are usually easier to run, simply because there is more time to recover below each stretch of rapids.

On the other hand, a river described as "technical" has many tight, rocky passages that require finely tuned skills to negotiate. A river with a sizable volume of water and large rapids is characterized as big water. Boaters here can expect rapids with intense hydraulics, but big water

Downriver Hazard

tends to be straightforward, lacking the complicated obstacles that make maneuvering difficult. Needless to say, beginning canoers have no business on either of these rivers.

RIVER HYDRAULICS
The key to running rapids requires an understanding of the river—its currents, form, and flow. Rapids are caused by a variety of factors, including physical aspects of the riverbed. The most obvious is the roughness of the riverbed, formed by rocks and boulders that have fallen from mountains and canyons or that have been swept into the main current by side streams. Also important are the gradient, volume, and constriction of the river.

Gradient
The gradient of the river, as it flows downstream, causes water to move faster, which normally renders rapids more difficult to maneuver. Gradient is typically measured by the number of feet per mile the river drops. Usually, the greater the drop, the more dangerous the river.

Exceptions exist. Many dangerous rivers, notably the Colorado River through the Grand Canyon, have mild gradients. This is because long stretches of calm water drop suddenly into tremendous rapids.

Volume

The volume of the river has a definite effect on its whitewater. A large volume increases the river's speed and the force of its rapids, which reduces the time you have to maneuver.

Generally, the greater the volume, the more difficult the rapids. But, again, this is not always the case. At low water, a rock may be clearly seen and avoided. At slightly higher levels, it may be possible to float over the rock, which has created only a small wave. At even higher levels, there may be a reversal that must be avoided. At still higher levels, the reversal may be completely washed out.

River volume is typically measured in cubic feet per second (cfs), the amount of water passing a point every second. This measurement is relative, of course: A smaller riverbed requires less volume for boating.

Add more water and you invariably increase the speed of the current. Changes in volume and velocity are important because water is heavy—8.33 pounds per gallon. A river flowing at a mere 1,000 cfs is backed by an incredible 62,400 pounds of force! This is the same force that moves huge boulders around the river with abandon. A boat held broadside against a rock is therefore placed in a precarious situation.

A river's volume can fluctuate greatly. Peak flows of snow-fed rivers typically occur during spring runoff. They decrease through summer and early fall, but increase quickly when it rains. When running unknown rivers, you should consult the proper sources about the latest volume and its suitability for boating.

Constriction

The constriction of the current also plays an important part in the river's difficulty. Constriction can result from either narrowing of the river banks or the presence of large boulders. It has the obvious effect of increasing the river's velocity, sometimes dramatically.

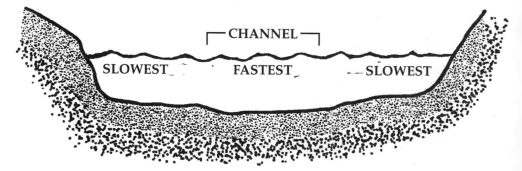

Cross Section of River Flow

SCOUTING RAPIDS

Always scout rapids whose path you cannot see clearly from the river, and stay alert for signs of major rapids ahead: noise, spray, an abrupt drop in the horizon line, a wall of boulders across the river, a narrow gorge.

To scout rapids, stop and walk downstream to get a closer look at what looms ahead. Look for obstacles and routes around them. You'll want to walk the entire stretch of rapids from shore if you're not familiar with it, or if the route isn't clear. It's much easier to look upstream and spot hidden rocks and reversals. Also check the end of the rapids to see where you'll finish, and to make certain there aren't more rapids below.

You'll need to look for prominent features to serve as mental markers when you make the run. Identifying those markers is important because of your perspective. From a high vantage point, the correct path seems obvious; but when you start into the rapids, you'll find yourself in a more confusing maze of foam and rocks.

After you've looked over the entire stretch and decided on a course, pause one last time at the top of the rapids. A second look at the entry is always a good idea. If other boaters are coming through, it's useful to watch them.

Depending on the configuration of the river, scouting from both shores may be necessary. Some boaters like to toss sticks into the river, to better judge where a current will take their boats. You need to spend enough time to be comfortable with your route. Always have an alternate route in mind, just in case something should go wrong with your first choice.

Scouting Rapids

71

TONGUE OF THE RAPIDS

When still water turns white, the current is usually fastest and deepest in the center—the tongue of the rapids. This is because friction between the water and a shallow riverbed slows the current. In deeper areas, the current is swifter and more powerful. This stronger current clears rocks away from the main channel, creating the characteristic V-shaped lead-in at the head of most rapids. This V typically points to the deepest and least obstructed channel. When there's more than one tongue, the best one will usually be the longest one or the one that drops more quickly.

Beware: The upstream V, with the tip of the V pointing upstream, is very different. It's a shockwave created by an obstruction lurking just beneath the surface, a warning to stay clear.

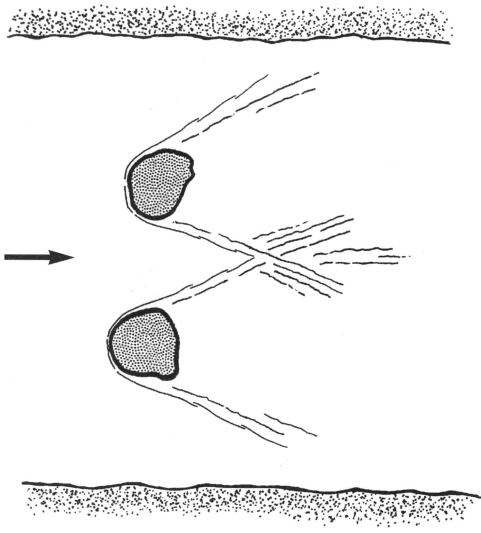

Tongue of the Rapids

BENDS

A river's tendency to meander causes erosion of its banks. As the current gradually carves out a new bend, it begins to pile up on the outside of the bend, and the inside of the bend becomes increasingly shallow. The deepest and fastest current is usually found along the outside of the bend.

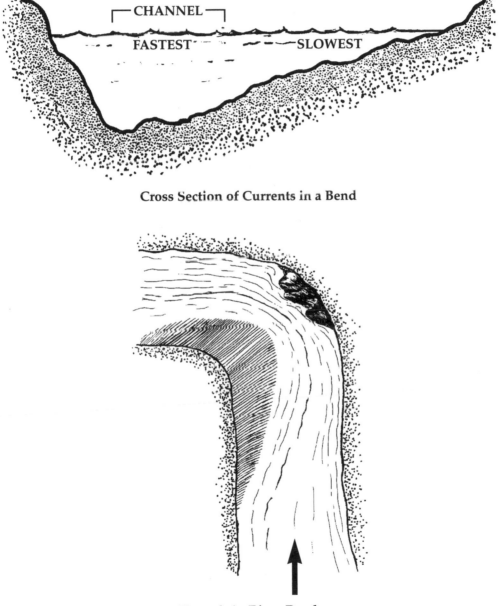

Cross Section of Currents in a Bend

Hazards in River Bends

EDDIES

Currents called eddies generally move upstream, either behind rocks or behind projections along the bank. The slack water on the inside of a bend is also referred to as an eddy, even though it doesn't move upstream.

The imaginary line between the main current and the eddy is known as the eddy fence, or eddy line, where the currents between the eddy and the main current mix and swirl. The eddy line can be very powerful, even capable of moving the boat back upstream.

Eddies are very useful for boaters entering or leaving shore, and they can often be used to stop the boat in midstream. Some eddies, especially those of the swirling, whirlpool variety, should be avoided because they are capable of trapping and rotating a boat.

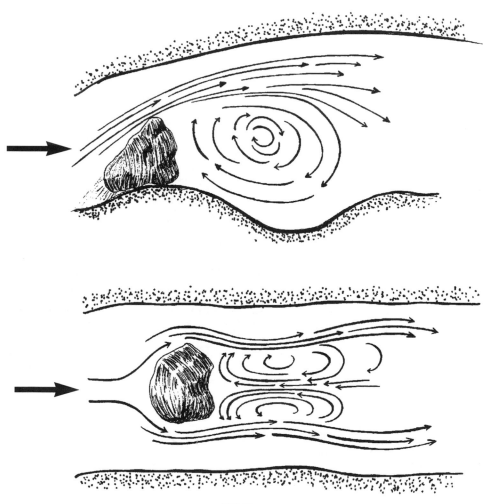

Eddies

ROCK RECOGNITION

Huge boulders peeking above the surface of the water are obvious. Low-lying rocks are more problematic. Those hidden boulders just below the surface of the water are sometimes called sleepers. Watch for the characteristics that signal them. Water piles up on the upstream side of a rock, creating a pillow, which may or may not cover the rock entirely. Look, too, for the roostertails shooting up above or behind a rock.

A series of waves tends to be regular in configuration, and rocks below the surface tend to upset the pattern. If the last wave in a series doesn't fit the pattern, a rock may be lurking underneath. Look closely, too, into the white froth for the glimpse of darkness that signals a rock.

PILLOWS

When the river's current collides with a rock, some of it forms an upstream mound, called a pillow. As the mound grows in size, it eventually spills over, creating a circulating force called a hydraulic. The pillow may deflect spray into the air, creating a roostertail.

Pillows should usually be avoided because they may conceal an undercut rock or ledge, allowing the current to dive underneath. These areas are especially dangerous because they can entrap a swimmer.

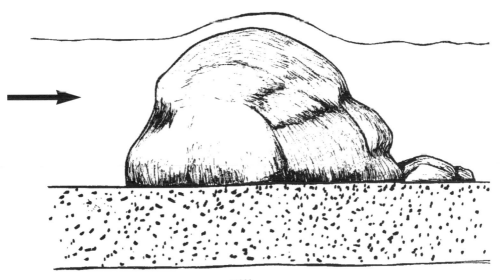

Pillow

REVERSALS

Rocks protruding above the surface of the river are obviously easy to spot. But when water flows over the top of a rock and into the slack water behind it, the water creates a backflow as it moves upstream and back on itself.

The movement of the current on the downstream side of a rock is generally known as a reversal. If the rock is deeply submerged, a large reversal—known as a hole—may develop.

Reversals come in various shapes and sizes. Knowing the difference between friendly and not-so-friendly holes is the boater's most important skill.

Small holes present little trouble. But there are holes that can stop a boat, appropriately called stoppers. Even larger ones—called keepers—can hold and recirculate a boat with ease; they can give a boater the proverbial "Maytag" treatment.

How do you determine when a wave is a reversal? When the rock is just under water, it may be difficult to spot from upstream because there's little turbulence. Try to look for a calm spot in the midst of turbulence. Usually the rock will deflect the current, and as a result, the water levels out as it sweeps over the rock. Viewing a reversal from shore often allows you to see rocks that aren't visible when you're on the river. Other rocks are concealed by spray and can be seen only with steady concentration.

In a hole's extreme form—a waterfall—water plunges downward to the riverbed. Within the chaos is a jumble of violent currents. As the current comes back toward the surface and repeats the cycle, not much is allowed to escape—including a boat or boater caught inside.

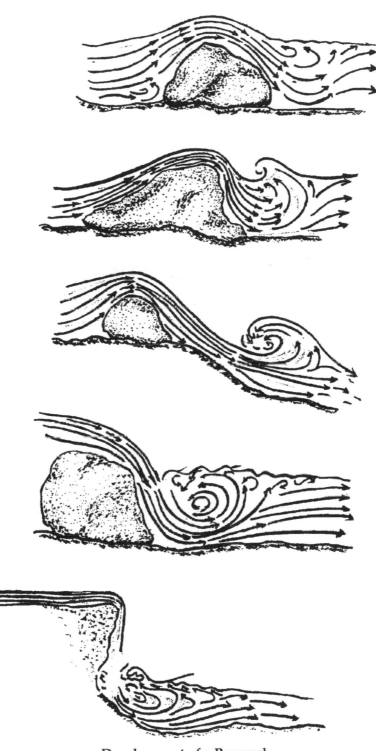

Development of a Reversal

STANDING WAVES

When fast currents are followed by slow ones, the water starts to pile up. If the change is gradual, there is turbulence in the form of standing waves. These are sometimes called wave trains, or if they're at the end of rapids, tailwaves. When standing waves converge, they surge randomly in a phenomenon called haystacks.

While standing waves are found in most rapids, they are usually too small to cause concern. If the wave is high but rounded, it's best to approach it bow first, allowing the boat to ride over the crest. If the waves are steep and angular, with a chance of overturning the boat, it's normally a good idea to move to the side, which is usually calmer than the center.

It is best, however, to first make sure that the waves are, in fact, standing waves. Rocks just below the surface can create mounds of water that first appear to be standing waves. Careful observation is required: Standing waves are regular and patterned, while waves concealing submerged rocks are usually more jumbled. These irregular waves, known as backcurlers, can overturn an unwary boater.

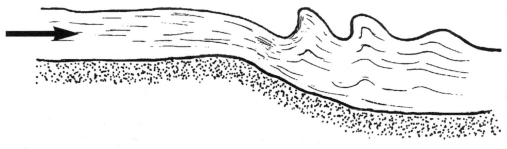

Standing Waves

SWEEPERS AND STRAINERS

During spring floods, rivers can carry a lot of debris: fallen trees, over-hanging branches, and logs wedged between rocks. River runners call these sweepers (downed trees that allow current to flow through but which may trap a boat or swimmer) and strainers (where the river filters through boulders). The force of water moving into such obstacles can present an extremely dangerous situation.

Sweeper

6

Tackling Hazards

Armed with a command of paddling strokes and the ability to recognize rocks and rapids, you're now ready to start tackling a few of these obstacles.

Again, it makes sense to start off slow and avoid hazards you're not quite ready for. The maneuvers described in this chapter are not difficult to execute, but they do take some time to practice—and perfect.

THE ENTRY
Selecting the proper entry into rapids is very important, because it often determines the rest of the run.

The V-shaped tongue at the head of most rapids typically points to the deepest and least obstructed channel. When there's more than one tongue, the best one will usually be the longest one or the one that drops more quickly.

As you approach the rapids, take one last look at where you're going. You may want to kneel, or even stand, in the boat for a better view. Once you've decided on the route, don't change your mind midstream unless you see something significant that you didn't spot earlier.

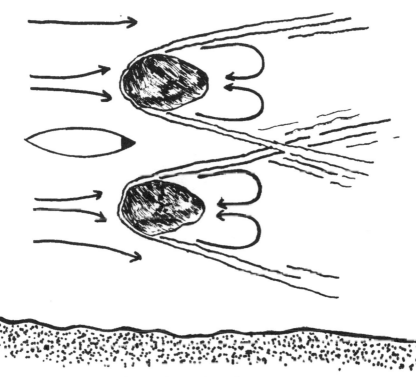

Proper Entry into the Tongue

THE FERRY
The technique for crossing a river is commonly known as the ferry, and there are several types.

Upstream Ferry
In the forward, or upstream, ferry, you point your canoe upstream and, with forward strokes, paddle against the current. Set your canoe at a thirty- to forty-five-degree angle to the current, with the bow pointing toward the shore you wish to travel to. In a tandem canoe, the stern paddler is responsible for setting and maintaining the proper angle to the current.

When you set an angle to the current and paddle forward, the forces applied against your canoe move you across the river. Varying your paddling force and/or the angle to the current will determine your final direction of travel.

The disadvantage to this method is that you have to look over your shoulder to see obstacles downstream.

Upstream Ferry

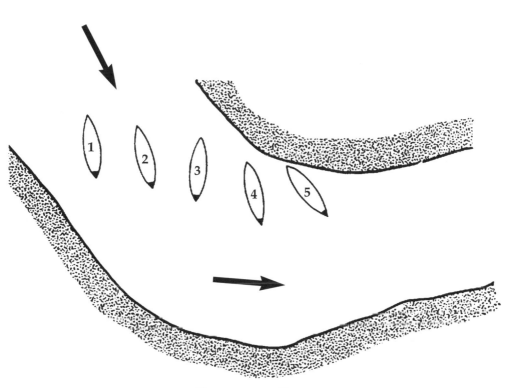

Downstream Ferry

Downstream Ferry

The downstream ferry, with the bow of the boat headed downstream, uses the power of the river's current and a forward stroke to move your boat across the river as you angle the bow toward the opposite bank. The angle is set and maintained by the bow paddler. With the back ferry, the bow is turned downstream as in the downstream ferry, only the paddle stroke is reversed. With the back ferry, you face the obstacle you want to avoid and backpaddle away from it. This technique allows you to see hazards downstream and to slow your speed in the current while moving laterally across the river. Unfortunately, the back ferry uses the much weaker back stroke.

Ferry Angle

You must adjust the ferry angle to account for the speed of the current and for how quickly you want to get across the river. To move across the river quickly, you should increase the angle of the canoe so that it is more perpendicular to the current. This increased angle, however, will increase the boat's speed downstream because there is more surface area to be moved by the current.

To slow the downstream speed of the canoe, decrease the angle so that the canoe is more parallel to the current and the surface area of the canoe in the current is decreased. This decreased angle, however, will not allow quick movement across the river.

Remember: The ferry angle is always relative to the current, not the river bank. A canoe may appear to be broadside to the bank, but have a proper ferry angle in relation to the current.

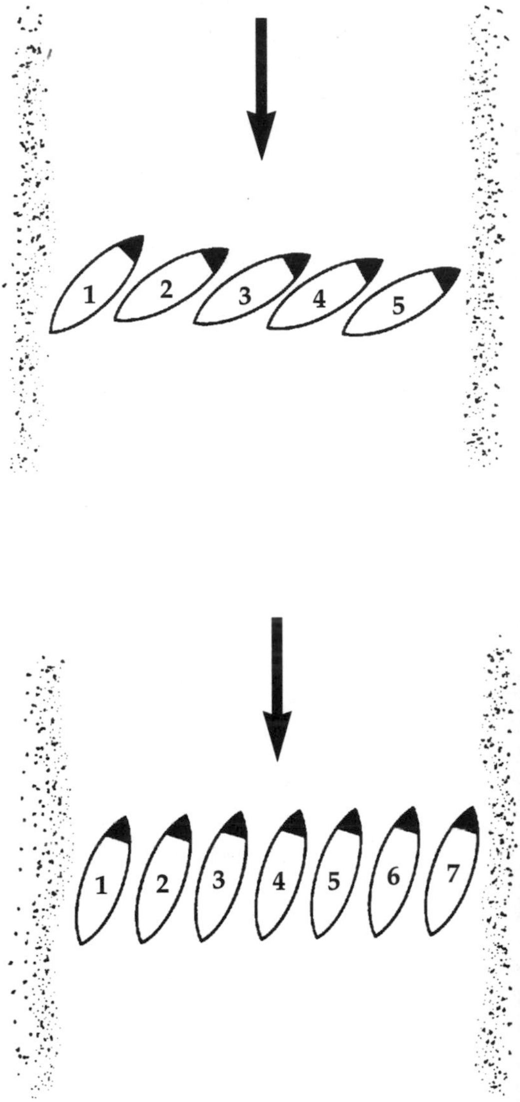

Ferry Angle

84

PARALLEL SIDE SLIP

An easy maneuver that can be used to avoid rocks in a slow-moving current is the parallel side slip.

The bow paddler picks the route through the rocks by moving the front of the canoe to the left or right. The stern paddler quickly moves the back of the canoe in the same direction, keeping the canoe parallel to the current.

The strokes used for this maneuver are the draw and the pry. The stern paddler counters with strokes opposite to those of the bow paddler. For example, the bow paddler, with a quick pry, points the front of the canoe in the desired direction until the middle of the canoe is past the obstacle. The stern paddler, with a quick draw, then straightens out the canoe so it is parallel to the current again.

The parallel side slip is effective only in a slow-moving current. As the current's speed increases, you must use a different maneuver. A canoe moving sideways, even slightly, makes a larger target for a rock.

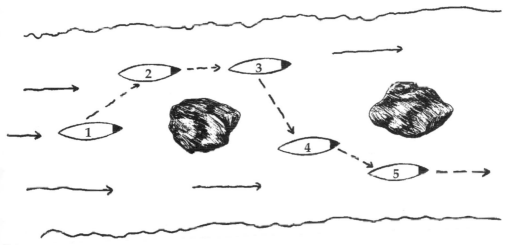

Parallel Side Slip

BENDS

Because the deepest and fastest current is usually found along the outside of a bend, the current has a tendency to move the boat there. Unfortunately, the outside of the bend often contains large boulders, overhanging trees, undercut cliffs, and other hazards.

It's best, then, to approach rapids on the inside of a bend, using the back ferry to slow your course downriver and allow you to see downstream. That way you can avoid the obstacles on the outside of the bend if they're present. If the outside is clear, you can then move to the deeper and faster current there.

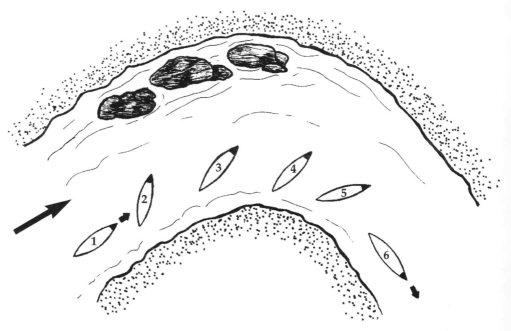

Negotiating a Bend

EDDY TURNS

Eddies often offer superb resting places in the river, and for this reason they are very useful to canoers. To paddle into an eddy you use a technique known as the eddy-in, and to leave an eddy, you use the peel-out.

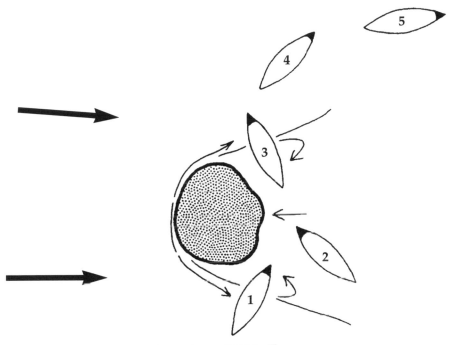

Overview of Eddy Turns

Entering an Eddy

To eddy-in, point your canoe toward the top (upstream end) of the eddy, starting well upstream of the eddy so that the current will not carry you past it. Paddle forward and enter the eddy with good forward momentum.

The moment the bow crosses the eddy line and enters the calm water in the eddy, your canoe will start to spin because of the current differentials. As the canoe spins, you must lean into the turn (i.e., upstream) to avoid overturning.

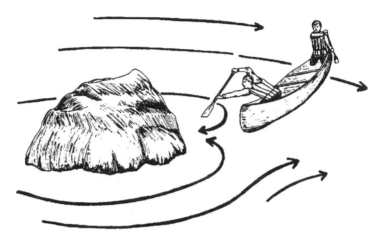

The bow paddler uses a high brace, and the stern paddler uses a forward sweep to enter an eddy.

The bow paddler uses a pry, and the stern paddler uses a low brace to enter an eddy.

Leaving an Eddy

The peel-out is the method used to leave an eddy. A similar maneuver to the eddy-in, it uses the same techniques of turning on the eddy line.

Paddle upstream in the eddy, and point the canoe so that it will cross the eddy line at a ninety-degree angle. It is important to have enough forward speed to carry you across the eddy line and into the current. Then, you must lean into the turn (i.e., downstream).

The bow paddler uses a high brace, and the stern paddler uses a forward sweep to leave an eddy.

The bow paddler uses a pry, and the stern paddler uses a low brace to leave an eddy.

AVOIDING ROCKS

Some rivers have rapids strewn with rocks and boulders, called boulder gardens or rock gardens.

Scout these rapids first so that you can plan a careful route through them. Be sure to use eddies that form behind rocks to assist your turns or slow your boat down.

It is best, of course, to anticipate upcoming rocks well in advance. If you're about to broach on a rock and you can't avoid the collision, lean toward the rock (allowing the current to flow underneath). If you follow instinct and lean away from the rock, the canoe could flip, fill with water, and become pinned against the rock. Fortunately, many boulders have a pillow on the upstream side, which tends to push you away from the rock.

RUNNING RAPIDS: A REVIEW

You've had a long, close look at the rapids below, either from the boat or from the shore. You've finally decided on your route through the whitewater maze. Now it's time for the run—and some fun!

Entry. The entry into rapids is the most critical maneuver of all. Many rapids, perhaps most, require very little maneuvering if correctly entered. The rapids you're entering will no doubt appear different from your new perspective on the water, so a last-minute look will be helpful.

The basic rule is to keep the boat headed directly into the waves of the rapids. A boat that's sideways to the current is infinitely more prone to overturning.

Holes. Knowing which holes to avoid is the essence of the river runner's art. Slowing one's speed downstream is essential, and this is typically accomplished through a series of ferry maneuvers across the river, moving the boat along the deepest and least obstructed channel.

If there are holes you can't avoid, try to punch through them as hard and fast as you can. This maneuver takes advantage of the current flowing downstream of the hole. Throwing your weight downstream may also help push through.

Bends. The ferry maneuver is especially important on a bend in the river. Currents, unfortunately, don't curve with the river's bends. Instead, they flow in a straight line from the inside of the bend to the outside. The river's tendency, as a result, is to move a boat to the outside of the bend. To avoid this, a boater must enter from the inside corner of the bend. It's easier to follow the current to the outside of the bend if the path is clear, rather than fight the current to the inside if it's not.

Eddies. In a stretch of violent whitewater, eddies can present havens of safety while you catch your breath or scout the rest of the rapids. Eddies allow for amazingly dramatic stops and turns. When entering or leaving eddies quickly, care is usually required to avoid tipping or even flipping the boat.

The further upstream in the eddy, the stronger the stopping force. If you need to stop quickly and positively, aim high in the eddy. Otherwise, you may miss it. Enter the eddy with a good angle and speed in order to pierce the eddy line, which is usually moving faster than the main current. Once you cross the eddy line, the upstream current will catch the boat.

Bailing. A boat can hold a lot of water, rendering it difficult to maneuver. On rivers with continuous whitewater, it's important to keep the boat as light as possible. The quickest way to empty a canoe full of water is to land the boat, climb out, and turn it upside down. If eddies are in short supply, bailing may be difficult if the next stretch of rapids is just downstream.

LOW-WATER TECHNIQUE

A river is generally less intimidating at lower water levels. There may be more obstacles to avoid, but the river is moving more slowly, allowing you more time to scout rapids and make decisions. Less volume means reduced power as well, so the river may be more forgiving.

On the down side, some rapids will have to be lined or portaged because there won't be enough water in which to maneuver, and constant rock-dodging can be tiring. Load the canoe lightly so it will be more maneuverable and easier to float over shallows.

To avoid the frustration of coming to a halt in shallow spots, look ahead for signs of shoals. If the river is clear, the color change alone may alert you to shallows. Watch the surface of the river and follow the waves. River current favors the high bank and the outside bend.

HIGH-WATER TECHNIQUE

Large rapids demand special skills. Don't attempt large-volume rivers until you're ready for them. The main problem with high water is the incredible force of the current. You'll need to scout big-water rapids carefully from shore, and if the water's cold, you should wear protective clothing.

Once on the river, you have to paddle hard into big waves so the canoe doesn't slide backwards. If you get knocked sideways by a powerful wave, correct your position immediately so the canoe doesn't flip. Keep a lookout for eddies, especially when scouting big rapids. These offer a safe landing place—a temporary haven from the rapids around you.

The greatest danger comes from reversals, which can swell to enormous proportions. If you find yourself in a large hole, head into the wave bow-first and paddle furiously. You'll need to generate enough speed to push through the wave and power your boat out of the hole.

Should you lose momentum, you'll feel the canoe sliding backwards. Brace hard downstream to keep the canoe upright. You may be able to catch the current below the surface with your paddle, and then propel the canoe free. The danger of reversals is that strong back currents can easily trap a swimmer, who is then recirculated until flushed out.

If you're caught in such a predicament, don't panic. The recirculating effect ends at the sides of the reversal; try to work your way out toward these sides if you can. If this fails, thrust your paddle below the surface to reach the forward-flowing current.

What about waterfalls? You may have seen photographs of canoes jumping falls. This is definitely not recommended. Even experts have suffered neck injuries, leaving them quadriplegics for life. It's simply not worth the risk.

SURFING WAVES

Surfing a river wave is much like riding an ocean swell, except that on a river, the waves are stationary and the water moves through them.

Look for waves that are regular in shape and form. Turn your boat to face upstream as you enter the waves, then paddle as hard as you can, straight upstream. When the boat stalls on a wave, you're surfing. A rudder stroke will keep your boat from slipping sideways.

WIND

Wind, of course, can be just as much a hazard on a lake as rocks and rapids are on a river. A few of the techniques described below will help you deal with the problems of winds.

Headwinds

The techniques for paddling into headwinds are important to keep the canoe from capsizing.

Before battling headwinds, study your map for possible windbreaks and resting spots. These might include the leeward shoreline, islands, or points of land. Plot a route that offers you the best wind protection and the most options for getting off the water if the wind should increase.

When you paddle into headwinds through large waves, you may need to lighten the bow so that it rises over the waves and takes in less water. This can be done by shifting gear toward the stern or putting the lighter paddler in the bow. Too light a bow can also be a problem, as it may catch the wind and be blown off course.

A little skill is required to hold a canoe on course while heading into the wind. To ensure forward progress, both paddlers need to paddle hard, with the stern paddler executing quick and effective correction strokes. If the stern paddler rudders, not only does he miss forward strokes, but the dragging paddle slows the forward momentum of the canoe.

As headwinds increase, so does the size of the waves. When the waves reach the point that they recirculate upon themselves, they are known as breaking waves and can be dangerous. The best tactic for dealing with breaking waves is to head directly into them. This will slow you down but will reduce your chances of capsizing. When whitecaps start to occur, it is time to get off the lake.

Crosswinds
Paddling crosswinds requires you to use another set of techniques. Even in a light crosswind, you can be blown sideways, and as the winds increase, so does the risk of capsizing. To avoid this possibility, you need to quarter the waves, which involves negotiating the waves at an angle. This angle is typically forty or fifty degrees, but in a strong wind, you will need to use a smaller angle to avoid your exposure to the wind. Remember to turn the bow into large breaking waves to avoid taking in water.

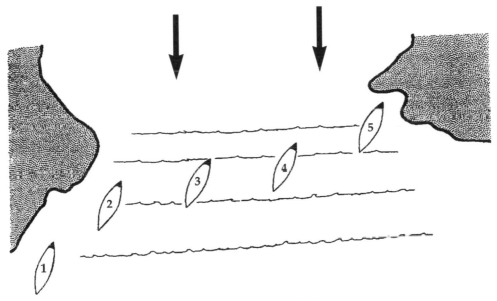

Negotiating Crosswinds

Tailwinds
You would think that paddling in a tailwind is helpful because the wind is behind you. This is true in light winds, but tailwinds can become a problem as they increase in strength. A large tailwind tends not only to lift the stern of the boat, but to push its bow into the wave ahead. As the wave picks up speed, it can pivot the canoe sideways. When this happens, you can easily turn over. To keep the canoe from turning sideways, use a strong rudder or draw stroke.

Staying Together
It's important for a group of canoers crossing a lake to stay together. An experienced paddler should stay in the lead to set the pace and choose a

safe route. It is also a good idea to have an experienced paddler at the rear of the procession in order to help those having difficulty.

LINING AND PORTAGING

If the decision is made not to run the whitewater ahead, you basically have two choices. You can guide the boat along the bank with ropes, a procedure called lining, or you can carry the boat around the rapids, an option known as portage. Portaging naturally involves a lot of work. Lining is easier, but it does take some practice to control the boat from the shore.

Lining

If you plan to do any lining, you will need to attach painters close to the waterline by using a lining bridle. Otherwise, when lining a rapid you will roll the canoe over when you pull it to shore. To install special lining painters in a plastic canoe, some boaters drill holes just above the waterline, glue in a piece of plastic tubing, and thread the painter through.

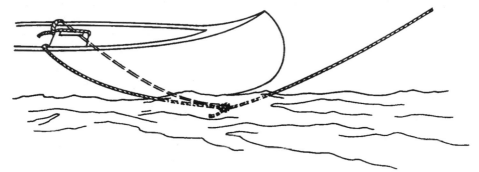

Lining Bridle

Lining a Rapid

Before lining, always lash down the gear (or remove it altogether). It is usually easier for two people to do the lining. The person with the bow line leads the boat downriver. The person with the stern line plays out the rope slowly, acting as brake and anchor to keep the canoe from getting out of control. In rocky stretches of the river, lining may be difficult because of tight maneuvering. In shallow areas, it's often necessary to have someone push the boat along or farther into the current, while others maintain control with lines attached to the boat. In sections of the river with powerful currents and no obstructions, the boat can be allowed to float freely, with lines attached but slackened, to the calm water below.

When lining a boat, always wear your life jacket.

Tracking
The opposite of lining is tracking, which involves moving the canoe upstream with lines. The process is practically the same, only it's a little more difficult because you're working against the current.

Portaging
There comes a time in every canoer's life when the inevitable must be faced—the portage. The technique of portaging the boat and gear is essentially the same whether you need to avoid a stretch of whitewater or simply move the canoe to the next lake.

Two-Person Portage

Two-Person Portage. Most canoers find that for long distances a canoe is best carried by two people, who hoist the boat upside down onto their shoulders. The canoe can rest on your shoulder, or you can tuck your head inside. The preferred method has the person in front outside the boat for better vision, while the rear person stays inside the boat for better stability.

One-Person Lift. When done correctly, one person can easily lift a canoe to portage it. Stand at the center of the canoe and roll the canoe away from you, by lifting the near gunwale with both hands. Bending your knees (with feet spread apart), lift the canoe up onto your thighs so the inside of the canoe is facing up.

Then move one arm to the far gunwale, keeping your other arm between your legs to cradle the canoe. With a rocking motion, swing and roll the canoe up and over your head. Place your head so that the carrying yoke lands squarely on your shoulders.

After the canoe is moved, the camping supplies and other gear can be carried to the boat. Most boaters move the canoe a few hundred yards and put it down. Then the rest of the equipment is brought to that point. This method gives you a chance to rest from hauling a heavy boat.

One-Person Canoe Lift

7

Safety

Until you've actually been there, it's difficult to imagine the force of a river pounding down on a boat out of control, or the danger of hypothermia if a paddler overturns in the middle of a lake. Like most outdoor pursuits, canoeing can be dangerous. But it's also true that most accidents can be prevented with a little foresight. A healthy attitude of caution is perhaps the best safety precaution of all.

WHITEWATER RATINGS
In the whitewater community, both rivers and individual rapids are rated according to their degree of difficulty.

The most common rating system, the International Scale of Whitewater Difficulty, uses a scale of Class I through Class VI, with Class I being easy water and Class VI being virtually unrunnable. Remember, though, that the ratings are subjective, and they may fluctuate wildly depending on drought or flood conditions and the seasonal water level. Here they are briefly described (see the chart for detailed descriptions):

- Class I: Very easy.
- Class II: Small and regular waves; good for beginners.
- Class III: Numerous waves large enough to cover the boat; some maneuvering required.
- Class IV: Difficult rapids; precise maneuvering required; high and irregular waves.
- Class V: Exceedingly difficult rapids; long, rocky stretches of violent currents.
- Class VI: Experts only; a serious risk to life.

A plus or minus sign is sometimes used to further refine the classifications (you may have, for example, a Class III+ or a Class IV-).

Another system, known as the Western Scale, is less commonly used, appearing mostly on maps of some rivers in the Southwest; it rates rapids on a scale of 1 to 10. Some boaters prefer this system because it is more precise.

Determining whether your skill level is adequate for the river's difficulty is crucial to a safe trip. Keep in mind, too, that rapids may be underrated. Experts, who are often rafters or hardshell kayakers, tend to underestimate rapids that would be very challenging for a canoer. Ratings can quickly change, especially with higher-than-normal water levels. A straightforward Class III at a medium water level can easily become a Class V should the river rise. A sweeper or strainer lurking in otherwise easy rapids can make for a very dangerous situation. A remote river requires a higher level of skill than one close to civilization. Cold water creates an additional hazard due to hypothermia.

Rapids with a maze of routes are more difficult than those followed by long, quiet pools where a boater can easily swim to shore. Rapids that follow one after another are obviously more dangerous than those with calm stretches in between.

Ratings should be regarded for what they are—guidelines subject to change. In some cases, rising water increases the rating. In others, the rapids become easier with higher water. Most rapids, however, are more difficult at higher levels, simply because the speed and force of the current are increased.

THE INTERNATIONAL SCALE OF WHITEWATER DIFFICULTY

CLASS I—Easy. Waves small; passages clear; obstacles easy to spot well in advance and avoid.

CLASS II—Novice. Rapids of moderate difficulty; passages mostly clear, some maneuvering required.

CLASS III—Intermediate. Waves numerous, high, and irregular. Rocks and eddies present. Rapids with clear passages, but may be through narrow spots, requiring expertise in maneuvering. Scouting may be necessary.

CLASS IV—Advanced. Long rapids; waves powerful and irregular. Dangerous rocks and boiling eddies. Passages difficult to scout; powerful and precise maneuvering required. Scouting mandatory first time. Risk of overturning or wrapping boat, and long swims for paddlers. For very skilled boaters.

CLASS V—Expert. Extremely difficult, long, and very violent rapids, following each other almost without interruption; riverbed extremely obstructed. Big drops; violent current; very steep gradient. Scouting mandatory but often difficult. Risk of boat damage and serious injury to paddlers. For teams of experts with excellent equipment.

CLASS VI—Extreme. Extraordinarily difficult. Extremes of navigability. Nearly impossible and very dangerous. For teams of experts only, at favorable water levels and after close study with all precautions.

PERSONAL PREPARATION

The best safety measures are preventive. Sharpening wilderness skills, staying in good physical condition, keeping equipment in good repair, and researching the territory you plan to cover are all important. Still, accidents do happen, even to the most experienced paddler, and being prepared just makes sense.

It's always a good idea to start on easy rivers early in the season to gain some experience before moving on to more difficult water. When running any river you're not familiar with, collect everything you can: guidebooks, maps, magazine articles, and reports from other boaters.

On the river, try to maintain a fairly relaxed pace, and be sure to allow plenty of time for scouting or lining rapids. It's also important to know the proper procedures for rescuing boaters and boats. Most river accidents don't happen on the river—they happen in camp. The consequences of your actions are certainly made more serious by remoteness.

Trip leaders. Those who lead trips have special responsibilities. They must collect maps and guidebooks, together with detailed information about the rapids. They must also be aware of changes in river level and how these will affect the run. They should review with the other boaters the safety and rescue matters—the hazards downstream, the order the group should travel, rescue stations, and signals to communicate between boats.

Leaders must also check the gear: life jackets, rescue rope, first-aid kit, repair materials, and survival equipment. They must give their plans to the appropriate authorities if rescue is needed. And they must determine points of assistance in case of emergency.

ADEQUATE CLOTHING

The advice about clothing is fairly straightforward: Always wear adequate clothing to protect against cold water and sunburn. Don't forget important accessories: proper foot gear, eyeglass retainers, sunglasses and a hat, a helmet on rocky rivers, and a wetsuit or drysuit on cold rivers.

The biggest threat presented by cold weather and water is hypothermia, the condition in which the body loses heat faster than it can be generated. Even with protective clothing, hypothermia can set in quickly. (See detailed discussion on hypothermia below.)

EQUIPMENT PRECAUTIONS

Making sure that your boat is in good working order is very important, especially on remote rivers. In the case of unfamiliar rivers, you should also make certain that your safety equipment is adequate.

PFD. The most indispensable piece of safety equipment, of course, is the life jacket. It must provide sufficient flotation for the water you will be tackling.

Rigging. Rigging the boat properly is critical to safety. You must eliminate any sharp projections that could possibly cause injury. Check to insure that nothing will cause entanglement if the boat should overturn.

Bailer. Carry a good bailing device, and make sure it's securely fastened to the boat.

Spare paddle. Always carry a spare paddle.

Rescue lines. In the case of rescue, plenty of rope is the key. For lining or boat rescue on difficult rivers, there should be at least fifty feet available in addition to that ordinarily used for bow and stern lines (carabiners will also come in handy).

Bailer

Throw rope. For rescue of boaters, the throw ropes made for that purpose are excellent because they float and can be easily tossed. (See the discussion on throw ropes later in this chapter.)

First-Aid Kit

First-aid kit. A good first-aid kit is imperative, especially on longer and more remote trips.

Repair kit. The repair kit should include repair materials for boats and other equipment such as paddles and stoves.

Helmet

Helmets. These days whitewater canoers are beginning to wear helmets, just like hard-shell kayakers. This is mostly because canoers are challenging tougher, rockier rivers where helmets provide an important measure of safety. On easier waters, helmets aren't necessary, but on more difficult whitewater, a helmet could save your life. The helmet you choose should be snug, but not so tight that it causes discomfort. The protective internal suspension is usually foam, but cheaper versions have plastic strapping. Whitewater helmets are designed with ear openings so you can hear upcoming rapids and warnings from fellow canoers.

River knives. Also helpful are whitewater safety knives. Most canoers wear these knives upside down on their PFDs so the knives are readily accessible. A serrated edge is more efficient for cutting ropes, and a double-edged knife is better yet.

River Knife

Group Travel

GROUP TRAVEL

Never boat alone. Most boaters travel in groups of two or more for greater safety. The boat with the most experienced paddler leads the way, determining the best route through rapids and waiting below as the rest of the paddlers come through. Another experienced boater should run a "sweep" boat behind the group to make sure everyone makes it through safely and no one is left behind. Each boater should keep the one behind her in sight at all times. Inexperienced boaters should never pass the lead boat.

Although normally staying close together, boaters should increase the distance between themselves while running rapids. Crowding together not only restricts maneuverability, but increases the chances of collision, as well as the chances of forcing a boat against an obstacle in the river. There should be sufficient distance between boats so that the first boater can stop immediately if she sees trouble. Group travel also works well for the rescue of passengers and boats if an emergency should develop. Each boater, after running the rapids, can establish a position for the rescue of those following.

SIGNALS

A set of hand or paddle signals, agreed upon at the beginning of the trip, can be helpful in communicating from boat to boat, especially where there is some distance between boats and the roar of rapids makes communication impossible.

Signals should be simple: hands or paddle outstretched horizontally for stop; a waved hand or paddle for help; and a hand or paddle outstretched vertically for all clear.

"HELP! EMERGENCY!"

"ALL CLEAR—PROCEED THIS WAY"

Signals

"STOP!"

"ALL CLEAR—PROCEED DOWN CENTER"

Signals

SWIMMING RAPIDS

Every paddler should know how to swim safely through whitewater. These are the basic safety rules:

Posture

- Hold onto your paddle (if you can) and get to the boat's upstream end. A boat full of water can otherwise pin you against an obstruction.
- Float on your back with your feet held high and pointed downstream. That way, your feet, not your head, will meet the obstruction first. Backpaddle with your arms for control.

Breathing

- Take a breath as you are carried into the trough of the wave. When the current lifts you to the crest of the wave, hold your breath. Depending on how large it is, the wave will probably come crashing over your head, inhibiting breathing for a few seconds.

Position

- Stay with the boat until you get your strength and can see a safe place to land.
- Swim to shore as quickly as possible.

Hazards

- If you're about to be swept into a fallen tree, face forward and try to climb up onto it so you aren't swept underneath and trapped.
- If you're headed for a big drop, tuck into a ball. This will protect your body if you hit the river bottom.
- Let go of your boat and any other gear if it drags you into a dangerous situation.
- Don't try to stand until the water is very shallow. If your feet get caught under a ledge or between two rocks, the current can knock you over and hold your head under.

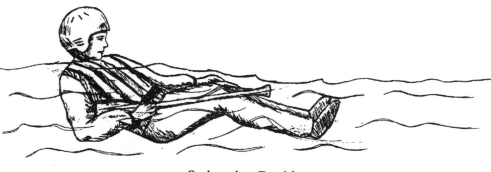

Swimming Rapids

Recirculating holes. Most holes are too small to be keepers. If a swimmer isn't flushed out immediately, he should try to swim sideways out of the hole. Large holes can recirculate a swimmer almost indefinitely. The best way to escape the force is to reach the powerful down-current. You can do this by tucking yourself into a cannonball position to avoid injury when you hit the riverbed, and then swimming hard to reach the deep currents moving downstream.

Strainers and sweepers. Some of the worst hazards of a river are currents that flow through sweepers and strainers. If a collision with a strainer or sweeper is inevitable, approach it headfirst, and the moment before you hit it, kick with your legs and try to pull your body over it. Do anything you can to avoid entrapment.

Climbing onto a Sweeper

HYPOTHERMIA

Hypothermia is the lowering of the body's temperature to a dangerous level. Any boater exposed to cold weather—and especially cold water—can become a victim. Symptoms of hypothermia typically include fatigue, apathy, forgetfulness, and confusion; shivering may or may not occur. Once the body is thrust into cold water, the brain begins to conserve body heat by constricting blood vessels in the arms and legs. Shivering usually (but not always) begins as the body attempts to generate heat. Then the body's core temperature starts to drop. As it falls below 95 degrees, there is difficulty with speech. Further decreases bring on muscle stiffness, irrational thinking, amnesia, and unconsciousness. Below a body temperature of 78 degrees lies death. In near-freezing water, the time from immersion to death can be as short as ten minutes!

HYPOTHERMIA SYMPTOMS

99-96 degrees F.   The body starts to shiver intensely and cannot be controlled. The victim cannot do complex tasks.

95-91 degrees F.   The victim still shivers violently. He has trouble speaking clearly.

90-86 degrees F.   Shivering decreases or stops and the victim cannot think clearly. The muscles are stiff but the victim keeps his posture. Total amnesia may occur. The victim usually can keep in psychological contact with the environment.

85-81 degrees F.   The victim becomes irrational, loses contact with the environment, and drifts into stupor.

80-78 degrees F.   The victim becomes unconscious and does not respond to the spoken word. The victim's heartbeat becomes irregular, and there are no reflexes.

below 78 degrees F.   Death will occur as the result of complications arising from failure of the cardiac and respiratory centers in the brain. These may include cardiac fibrillation and pulmonary edema. There is hemorrhage in the lungs.

Treatment

Awareness of the causes of hypothermia and the speed with which death can result is the most important aspect of prevention. Treatment is simple, but the sooner the better. First, replace wet clothes with dry ones, and then move the person into a warm shelter. If the person is unable to generate his own body heat, rewarming is required. Hot liquids may help, but never give him alcoholic drinks (which dilate blood vessels, allowing even greater heat loss).

Heat from a supplemental source should also be provided. If it's impossible to build a fire, body heat from others (lightly clothed for best results) is helpful. If the person loses consciousness, the situation is extremely serious, and hospitalization is required as soon as possible.

Hypothermia can be prevented, to a large extent, by adequate clothing, proper food, and good physical conditioning. The best clothing is a wetsuit or drysuit. The food you eat is also important: Sugar and carbohydrates are quickly oxidized to provide heat and energy.

SELF-RESCUE

If you should go overboard, the most important rescue technique to know is self-rescue. First of all, there may be no one else around. And even with other paddlers around you, it's easier and faster for you to rescue yourself than to depend on someone else.

Most important, don't panic. Hold onto your paddle, because you're going to need it once you're back in the boat. Next, look for your boat. In most cases, it will be right next to you.

Now is when handholds attached to the boat come into play. The bottom of the canoe will be smooth and slippery, and therefore difficult to hold onto. But the painters at the bow and stern will offer good handholds.

Once you grab the canoe, you will need to turn it upright. If the boat is empty, you may be able to turn it over in the middle of the river or lake. If the boat is loaded, you will probably have to swim the boat to shore.

Pulling the Swamped Boat to Shore

Getting back into an upright boat is a matter of pulling yourself over the side. Put the paddle inside first. If you're on a river, approach the boat from the upstream side, to avoid being pinned between it and a rock. If you can't get back into the canoe, you will still want to keep the boat downstream so there's no chance of being wedged between it and a rock. If you can't reenter the boat in the river, pull it to shore or into an eddy.

Don't try to stand up in a moving current, even if the water is shallow, because it can easily knock you over. Your feet could then become pinned under a rock, and if the current pushed your head under water, you could drown in a few feet of water.

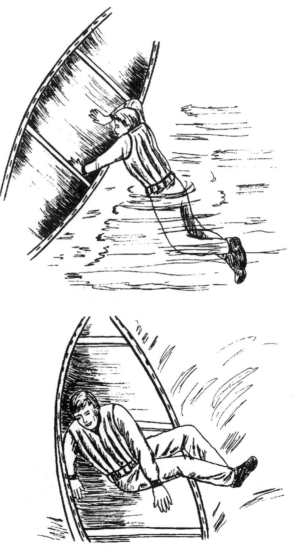

Getting Back into the Boat

RESCUE OF OTHERS

It's important for all river runners to know the proper techniques for the rescue of boaters and boats. Because the subject is extensive, the book *River Rescue*, by Les Bechdel and Slim Ray, is strongly recommended.

When running rivers with powerful currents, it is always advisable to have safety lines downstream for the rescue of those who may be unable to swim ashore.

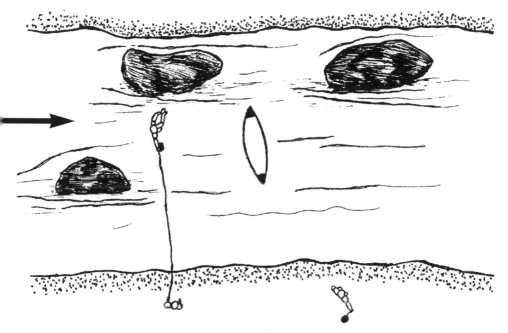

Rescue Stations

A number of throw ropes made specifically for river rescue are now available. These lines come in nylon bags with one end of the line attached to the bottom of the bag. You simply hold the end of the line and throw the entire bag, which feeds out like a spinning reel.

Throw Rope

111

If a second throw is necessary, the rescue line is first coiled. One-half of the coil is held in either hand. Half is thrown with an underhanded motion, and the other half is allowed to feed out freely (with the end held securely in the hand, of course).

The line should be thrown slightly downstream from the swimmer's position, since the swimmer is moving along with the current. After the swimmer grabs the rescue line, a tremendous pull will be exerted on the line. The rescuer should belay the line around a tree or around his waist, after making sure that the rescue path is free of sweepers, boulder gardens, and other hazards.

Tossing the Line

After the swimmer grabs the rope, he should turn on his back, face up. This allows his body to plane toward the surface and offer less resistance. The rope should never be wrapped around any part of the body.

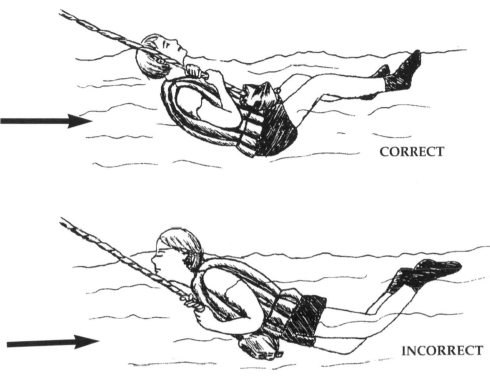

Rescued Boater's Positions

ENTRAPMENT
The combination of river current and an entangling object can prove fatal. Boaters on moving water must be alert for possible entrapment situations: sweepers and strainers, loose ropes, and undercut rocks.

Never tie yourself into a boat on moving water. When being rescued by a throw line, or when swimming whitewater, never wrap or tie a rope around any part of your body. Secure all loose lines, and have cargo tied down with straps that are just long enough to do the job (without any extra length hanging loose). Carry a whitewater safety knife.

RESCUE OF BOATS
In shallow rivers, the boat may become lodged on a rock or gravel bar, and it's normally easy to simply push it off the obstacle. But if the boat should collide with large boulders that protrude above the river's surface, a more serious situation may occur.

If the canoe is headed toward a large boulder, it is usually best to strike it with the bow of the boat. That way, the current of the river, with the aid of a few paddling strokes, will invariably swing the boat off the rock.

PINNING

A sideways collision with a rock—known as pinning—is more problematic, but a few quick precautions may prevent it.

Since a rushing current tends to pull the upstream side of the canoe under the current, fill it, and eventually submerge it, you should lean to the downstream side of the boat. This lifts the upstream side of the canoe out of the water, allowing the current to flow underneath. Be wary of entrapment, and be prepared to abandon the boat if necessary.

If the unavoidable happens and the boat pins itself against a rock, several methods should be attempted until one of them succeeds. First, shift your weight to the side of the boat most likely to spin off the rock. It may even be possible to then manually push the boat away from the rock. If that fails, try placing a paddle into the main flow of the river to act as a lever that will catch the force of the current and pull the boat off the rock.

Freeing a Pinned Boat

WRAPPING

If the canoe's upstream side is pulled completely underwater, a more serious situation presents itself. This unfortunate occurrence is known as wrapping the boat.

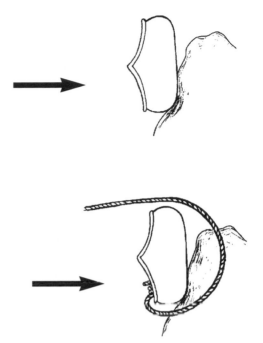

If the canoe is wrapped on a rock, but not seriously so, it may be possible to stand on the rock and pull the boat up and out of the water. If this isn't possible, or if it doesn't succeed, you'll have to attach lines to the canoe's bow and stern and then pull with all your might from shore.

A variety of intricate retrieval systems (beyond the scope of this book) have been developed by professionals to utilize mechanical advantage in retrieving boats. See the book *River Rescue*, by Les Bechdel and Slim Ray, for all the details. If all else fails, you may have to abandon the boat (secured to shore, of course) until lower water levels allow easier access.

Close-up of Rescue Rope

Freeing a Wrapped Boat

RETRIEVING CANOES

This maneuver is used to get water out of a swamped canoe by pulling it up and over a rescuing canoe.

Meet your partner in the middle of the rescuing canoe. Face each other and kneel down for better stability. Grab the end of the swamped canoe, and lift it (still upside down) up onto the gunwale. Then pull it up and across your canoe. When both ends of the swamped canoe are out of the water, flip the canoe right side up, and then slide it back into the water.

Retrieving the Canoe

EMERGENCY GEAR

You should carry basic emergency gear and know how to use it. Each canoe should have a spare paddle and also carry a throw rope for rescuing swimmers and rescue lines for lining and pulling boats off rocks. You'll also need a good repair kit and a good first-aid kit. Individual paddlers, especially in cold weather or wilderness situations, should carry some kind of survival kit on their PFD, with a fire starter, waterproof matches, a rescue carabiner, and a signal whistle. Most canoers who run whitewater carry a whitewater safety knife attached to their PFD to cut an entangling rope.

GETTING HELP

Should a serious injury occur on the river, remain calm and treat the injured person to the best of your ability. If you're close to civilization, perhaps someone can walk to the nearest road. If there are other paddlers on the river, ask them to go for help.

8

Overnight Trips

The paddling trip had been planned for months, and we would soon be leaving on a two-week journey through the Boundary Waters Canoe Area. The last-minute details remained, as they always do, but the trip would ultimately justify our efforts.

SEASONS

Peak runoff is the time when rivers have their highest flows. In dry years, the peak may not mean much, but it usually means high water, often running at dangerous levels.

As a result, the river courses through trees and bushes, places to stop are few, there's less time to make decisions, the powerful current is less forgiving, and the water is cold.

On smaller rivers, the peak may only last a few days, and the river eventually drops to a point where it's too low to run. This commonly happens on rivers in the East or small rivers with dry drainage areas. On these rivers, the season is limited to a few months in the spring or to the days following a rainstorm. In the West, larger rivers usually have a big peak, then drop slowly throughout the summer.

The challenge on smaller rivers with short seasons is to learn the optimum times to run them. Good guidebooks often supply this information, but the best source is boaters who run the river often.

INITIAL PLANNING

The initial planning for a canoe journey starts with an idea that eventually blossoms into a full-blown trip, with all the planning and provisioning that such an endeavor entails. A number of decisions will have to be made along the way, the first of which is in how luxurious a style you wish to travel.

Camping Styles

Camping styles vary. Equipment on luxury canoe trips consists of just about anything you can take on a car-camping trip. Large tents, bulky sleeping bags, and even cots can be carried if you like. Meals on these trips can be elaborate affairs. Fresh vegetables, fruits, and meats can be packed in coolers, and cooking done in cast-iron pots and pans. Some canoers take lawn chairs to relax by the water, and others even bring volleyball sets.

The equipment you pack will depend on the style you choose. Obviously, luxurious trips with fresh food and lots of equipment require more extensive planning.

Longer Trips

Longer canoe trips naturally involve more advance planning. Some require preparation weeks, even months, in advance. Because such a trip demands more preparation, let's take a closer look at some things to do when planning a longer trip.

Regulated rivers. Some areas have become so popular that the number of boaters is causing environmental problems: Vegetation is trampled, campfire scars abound, and disposal of human waste presents sanitation problems.

To minimize this impact, some government agencies have developed regulations to protect the land, including systems where you have to apply in advance to obtain a permit to run the river or camp along the lake (often a lottery is held). You'll want to write in advance: Six months to a year isn't too early for the most popular sites. Information about permits is found in most guidebooks and sourcebooks.

Assembling the party. A canoeing group can range from one friend to a dozen or more companions. Smaller groups involve fewer planning hassles, and in many cases, there's less damage to the environment. Some areas managed by government agencies may require you to keep the party within a certain size. Regardless of group size, everyone should be sufficiently experienced for the trip you're about to undertake.

Dispersing information. Get your party together far in advance of the trip. Talk over dates, equipment, costs, and so on. Delegate duties, and put someone in charge of renting or borrowing additional boats and assembling other group gear.

Preparation day. Some canoe parties tack on an extra day at the beginning of the trip to spend time in town buying food, packing vehicles, and so on.

Length of trip. Find out how long it normally takes to make the trip and adapt this to your plans. Give yourself plenty of leeway. The actual time will depend on many factors, such as how high the water is, the direction of the winds, and the number of portages.

CANOEING WITH CHILDREN

With careful planning, canoe camping can be enjoyed by the entire family. When you bring children along, there are some important points to keep in mind:

- Choose easy rivers and lakes with little possibility of capsizing a boat.
- Teach your children not to be afraid of water, and start them swimming at an early age.
- Let children help with repairs and general maintenance of the boats.
- Make the first trip a short one; a couple of hours is best.
- Always have children wear life jackets (wear yours to set a good example). Use one that will provide good buoyancy and will keep a child's head upright in water. Teach children how to fasten the jacket, and be sure there's no way they can slip out of it. Before the trip, have them swim in a pool with their jacket on.

TRANSPORTATION

If you're planning a lightweight trip, transporting equipment may not present much of a problem. For luxurious trips, getting to and from the river can be more complex:

- Cartop racks can be used to carry canoes on the smallest of cars; a sturdy rack can be used for other gear as well.
- Pickup trucks, vans, and other sport utility vehicles are useful, but be careful not to load them beyond their recommended limits.
- Trailers can be rented or borrowed and are especially helpful for transporting a number of canoes.

On trips where vehicles are subjected to much wear and tear, you might consider reimbursing the vehicles' owners. It may also be a good idea to caravan in case car trouble develops. One last comment: Be sure everyone knows exactly where they're going.

CARTOPPING

With the sophisticated line of cartop carriers available, even the smallest subcompact can transport a canoe. The accessories for these racks are impressive, and you'll no doubt find the setup that fits your needs perfectly. In any event, make sure the canoe and gear are securely attached to the rack before you hit the highway.

SHUTTLES

By their nature, river trips start at one point and end at another, so somehow you must shuttle your vehicles. The easiest solution, no doubt, is to hire a commercial shuttle driver. To find one, contact the nearest chamber of commerce or the government agency managing the river.

You can do your own shuttle by leaving a vehicle(s) at one end and the other vehicle(s) at the other end. This works well if there's not too much distance involved and you have plenty of time. Shuttles can involve an infinite variety of combinations, but the most common are the following:
- Drive to the take-out and leave one vehicle there. Then, in the other vehicle, everyone drives to the put-in.

- Drive to the put-in and unload all the people and gear. Then drive the vehicles to the take-out. Leave all but one of the vehicles at the take-out and return all the drivers to the put-in.

Either way, you'll naturally have to retrieve the vehicle at the put-in after the trip is over.

In performing a shuttle, make it clear to the others where you've put your car keys. Some people bring along two sets and keep them in separate boats in case of an upset. Others hide the keys on the vehicle so that the keys and vehicle are always together (be sure to hide the keys well). Also, be sure you don't accidentally leave the keys to the take-out vehicle at the put-in vehicle!

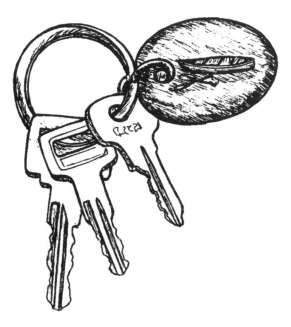

One last note about shuttles and driving. Many consider driving to be the most dangerous part of a canoe trip, because vehicles are heavily loaded, drivers are sleepy, and everyone is anxious to get on the water. Whenever you drive, use care and caution.

WATERPROOF CONTAINERS
A wide assortment of waterproof bags and boxes now are available for canoers, and the only problem is the final selection.

Waterproof Bags
Most boaters seem to prefer the soft surfaces of bags whenever possible. Not just for the obvious impact reasons, but because a bag expands and contracts to fit its contents and the space where it has to be squeezed.

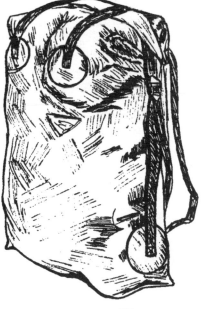

Waterproof Bag

Waterproof Box

Waterproof Boxes

Waterproof boxes have their uses. A camera box is an obvious example, and the kitchen box and toilet are others. Surplus ammunition boxes first come to mind; they make inexpensive, totally waterproof boxes. But many boaters prefer plastic because it's lighter and doesn't have the sharp edges of metal.

PACKING THE CANOE

Efficient packing begins with checklists (see Appendix 1 for samples). After several trips, you'll no doubt develop your own. Carefully going through a list is the best—and only—way to make certain nothing is forgotten or left behind. A trip can be ruined if someone should show up at the put-in of a wild river without a life jacket, or if everyone should arrive in camp to discover that no one remembered to bring matches.

How gear fits into the canoe depends on the individual boat and the preferences of the person loading it. In general, though, you'll want to put as much of your gear as possible into one large waterproof bag. One large bag will hold more than several smaller ones, and there's the added advantage of having only one waterproof seal to worry about. It's also easier to secure just one bag to the boat.

The drawback to one bag is finding that certain item you happen to need at the moment. To alleviate frustration, try to pack with unloading in mind: Place toward the bottom of the bag those camp items (like the tent and sleeping bag) that you'll need that evening, and toward the top of the bag the warm clothing or rain gear you'll need during the day.

Many canoers carry a smaller "day bag" where they can stow clothing and other items they'll want before camp—camera, sunglasses, suntan lotion, gloves, and so forth. Keep a water container handy, too.

When you pack the canoe for the first time, or if you're trying a different load, test it at home first to make sure everything fits. It's frustrating to arrive at the water and discover either that half of your gear won't fit, or that you left behind something that would have fit after all.

To properly rig a canoe with camping gear, keep the heavy items low and in the middle of the boat. The load should also be balanced as evenly as possible on both sides of the boat. None of the baggage should protrude from the sides of the boat, and the gear should not interfere with paddling.

Before you tie down the load and head out, take a short test run. If it doesn't feel right, paddle back to shore, rearrange it, then try again. Have another paddler check the waterline of your boat. Before you hit the water, you'll want everything in order.

When securing their load, many canoers prefer straps and bungee cords instead of ropes. With straps, you don't have to remember knots. Straps are easier to unfasten, and they cinch down tighter with less effort.

Always tie or strap in everything. That way, nothing will be lost, even if the boat capsizes. And don't leave any loose ends of ropes or webbing that could entangle you should the boat overturn.

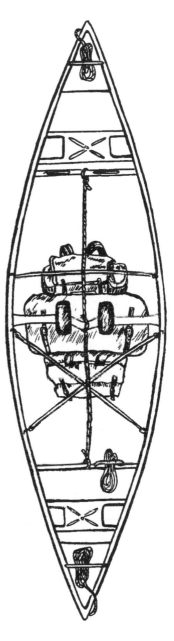

KNOTS

For many canoers, knots are an integral part of canoeing lore, and there's added satisfaction in being able to tie various knots from memory. There are a surprising number of books dedicated to the subject, but one recommended resource on this topic is *The Book of Outdoor Knots,* by Peter Owen. The following are a few basics to get you started.

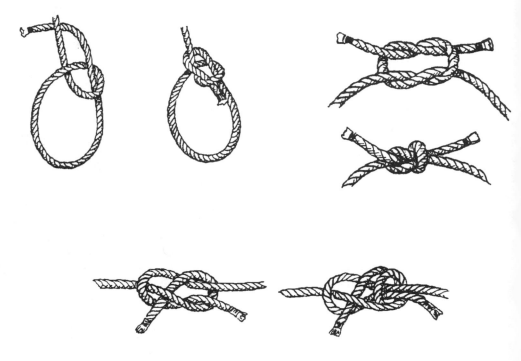

GARBAGE

Canoers tend to be protective of the path they paddle, which is fortunate for those of us who follow. It may be that canoers are more likely to appreciate the natural world they're escaping to—or less likely to spoil the beauty it took so much effort to reach. Whatever the reason, it's important to tread lightly on a resource that can be loved to death.

In the total scheme of things, what difference does one candy bar wrapper thrown to the wind make? The answer is a lot, especially when the single effect is multiplied, as it invariably is.

The rule for disposal of garbage is simple: Carry it all out. The best method for doing so is a plastic bucket with an airtight lid or perhaps a plastic garbage bag placed inside a more resilient nylon bag. Keep a small bag handy for use during the day, and be careful to collect even the smallest piece of paper.

If you're using a campfire or charcoal briquettes, burn all trash possible, but remember that aluminum foil packets will not burn and that certain foods (such as egg shells) require more time than a short morning fire. If the garbage can't be burned, dispose of it by placing everything except liquids in the garbage bag (grease, in particular, should always be carried out).

Liquid garbage, such as coffee, soup, and dishwater (containing biodegradable soap), should be strained first. The solids remaining can then be thrown into the garbage bag. In wooded areas (which foster quick decomposition), the liquid can be poured into a single hole dug for that purpose (but at least a hundred feet away from any area normally used for camping). In wooded areas that are heavily used, it may be better to pour the liquids into the main current of the river, where they will quickly disperse — but first check with the government agency managing the river. In desert regions (which don't foster quick decomposition), the liquid should always be poured into the main current of the river.

One way to avoid garbage in the first place is to plan ahead: Select foods and packaging that will result in as little trash as possible.

THE CAMPFIRE

Staring into the flames of a campfire is for many canoers the ideal way to end a day of paddling in the wild. But in some areas, fires have left scars that will take decades or more to heal, and trees have been stripped of their branches (and even cut down) to provide firewood. Even collecting deadwood can damage the environment if not enough is left to replenish the soil with nutrients and to provide shelter for birds and animals.

One alternative to the problem is to ban campfires and to use only stoves for cooking. Doing so would certainly eliminate fires, but it would also take some of the pleasure out of wilderness travel. Most ecology experts agree that a complete ban isn't necessary. It is important, however, to treat fires as a luxury and ensure that they have the smallest impact possible.

Fires may have to be banned, for example, when dry conditions render the fire risk high. Such regulations seem restrictive, but they prevent further destruction. Fires, officially permitted or not, are inappropriate in some areas anyway. In particular, fires should not be lit near and above the timberline, because of the slow growth of trees and the soil's need to be replenished by nutrients from deadwood.

In other areas, fires can be lit even on pristine sites without much harm to the environment, as long as you take certain precautions. You should leave no sign of your fire, and if possible, use a firepan (discussed in detail below). Do not leave behind partially burnt wood. If you don't use a firepan, refill the shallow pit you've created with sod or dirt removed when it was dug; spreading dirt and loose vegetation over the site will help conceal it. The ideal place for fires is below the flood level along rivers, since any traces will eventually be washed away.

Do not build a ring of rocks around a fire—the campsite soon becomes littered with blackened rocks. Although the idea is to contain a fire, the best way to do that is to clear the area of flammable materials; a couple of feet is usually large enough. You should also make sure there are no low branches or tree roots above or below the fire. Pitch your tent and other gear well away, preferably upwind, so sparks can't harm them.

If you camp at a well-used site with many rock-ringed fireplaces, use an existing one rather than make a new one. Take time to dismantle the other fire rings, removing any ashes and charcoal as garbage. Some designated backcountry sites provide metal fireboxes, and when present, they should be used.

If you collect wood, do so with care. First and foremost, do not remove wood—even deadwood—from living trees; deadwood is needed by wildlife and it adds to the site's attractiveness. Nothing is worse than a campsite surrounded by trees stripped of their lower branches and a ground bare of any fallen wood. In high-use areas, search for wood farther afield. Collect only what you need, and use small sticks that can be broken by hand—and easily burned to ash.

Firepans

If you build fires, seriously consider bringing a firepan—a metal container with three- or four-inch sides to contain fire and ashes. They're often required by the government agency managing the area, and they're the best way to contain ashes and prevent fire scars. If the firepan doesn't have legs, set it on rocks so it doesn't scorch the ground.

On large-volume or silty rivers, the ashes can be disposed of by dumping them into the main current of the river. If you deposit them in an eddy by the camp, the ashes eventually wash back to shore, soiling the beaches. Some campsites have become so littered that the soil has turned black. To prevent this, boaters should dump ashes where the current is strong and will quickly disperse any trace. Better yet, you can store the ashes as garbage and carry them out. To prepare ashes for storage, moisten them until they're cool and then shovel them into a container (an old surplus ammo can is ideal). At the next camp, dump the ashes out of the container and into the firepan before starting the fire. As the ashes are burned again at each camp, they are gradually reduced to a fine dust.

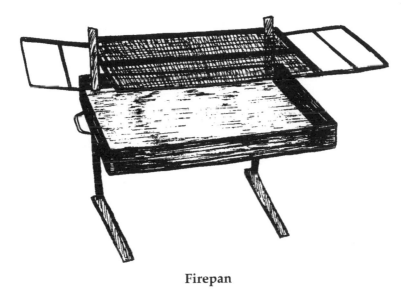

Firepan

If possible, locate the firepan near the river, so high water can clean away any small coals that are accidentally dropped. An additional safety tip for removing firepans: Throw a little water on the ground as soon as the pan is removed, because the ground below can burn bare feet.

Fires without Firepans
If you must build a fire without a firepan, build it where it will have less impact: either below the high-water mark on a rocky shoreline, or in a bare spot where it's easy to remove all remains.

Build as small a fire as you can. An entire meal can be cooked with amazingly little wood. When you're finished with the fire, thoroughly douse it with water and restore the site to its former condition. Throw any blackened rocks into the river.

DISHWASHING

If you're cooking with a camp stove and a single pot, washing dishes is a simple proposition. On luxurious trips with numerous pots, plates, cups, and silverware, the best procedure is a three-bucket wash. In the first bucket add very hot water with biodegradable dishwashing soap. Use the second bucket for rinsing, and the third bucket, with a capful of Clorox in it, for disinfecting dishes. It seems involved, but it works quickly and prevents intestinal problems that can occur from contaminated dishes.

Never dispose of dishwater, leftover food, or soap in side streams or the main river unless you're in the desert or advised to do so by the government agency managing the river. On a few rivers, such as the Colorado, there's less environmental impact if the dishwater is first strained of any solid food particles or coffee grounds (which are packed out as garbage), and then disposed of in the main current (not the eddies), rather than on land. Note: Use this procedure only on rivers where it is specifically recommended.

On other rivers, the best disposal method is to dig a small hole, carefully removing any sod. Use this same hole for all dishwater (the soil elements will quickly cause its decomposition). The hole should be situated away from the camp and above the high-water mark. When you're ready to leave, fill in the hole, pack down the soil, and replace the sod so that the hole is indistinguishable from its surroundings.

Dishwashing

HUMAN WASTE DISPOSAL

Solid human waste presents both an environmental impact and a hazard to human health. As a result, many government agencies now require it to be carried out. It's inevitable that the system will be implemented on most government lands, and it's a good idea in all heavily traveled areas. The cheapest, most convenient, and most effective means of containing and transporting this waste is in an airtight toilet box sold by various camping supply companies. The necessary items include the following:

- Metal toilet box approximately 18" x 14" x 8" in size (surplus ammunition boxes work well if they're airtight)
- Toilet seat
- Chemical deodorant or chlorine bleach
- Toilet paper, water dispenser, and hand soap

The system is easy to set up. Pour a small amount of the chemical deodorant or chlorine bleach into the toilet box and place the toilet seat on top (the water dispenser and hand soap can be situated nearby). Plastic bags should not be used with this system because they are not biodegradable.

Chemical deodorant or chlorine bleach is important because it reduces bacterial growth and the production of methane gas. The amount of chemical deodorant needed depends on the type used: A few ounces a day of liquid deodorant is sufficient for six or seven people, whereas approximately twice as much chlorine bleach is required for the same number of people. The number of toilet boxes needed depends on the number of people and the length of the trip; on average, it's possible to containerize a week-long trip for ten people in one box. After the trip, the waste should be deposited in an approved solid-waste landfill.

Side hikes also require sanitary waste disposal, but of a slightly different kind. To reduce impact, bury the waste (after carefully burning the toilet paper) in a hole about six inches deep, the best depth for soil elements that cause rapid decomposition. Carry a small backpacker's trowel, and make the hole at least a hundred feet from the river's high-water line and away from any area normally used for camping.

AFTERWORD

A journey by canoe is a passage from one life to another. You leave the noisy and predictable routine of the metropolis for the quietude and uncertainty of nature. The deeper you paddle into this world, the more your perspective changes. You see new things, of course, but you hear, smell, and feel them with an intensity you never thought possible.

These impressions quickly become indelible. Living in the fast pace of a big city, I sometimes can't remember what happened that morning. Yet images of canoe trips I took a decade ago are so crystal clear it seems as if they happened yesterday.

I vividly recall an alpine lake whose banks seemed to heave straight toward the heavens. Sunshine streamed into the narrow gorge to warm the white beaches spotted with lichen-stained rocks. Side canyons, filled with ferns and berry bushes, occasionally pierced the chasm to allow creeks to flow through. Along the shore lived deer, elk, bighorn sheep, and mountain goats. High above flew ospreys and bald eagles.

I remember paddling the wind-swept ridges and crags of a desert stream. There the gentle flow of the river piled itself against precipitous cliffs, where light danced upon the swirling surface. The air was as dry and brittle as the canyon that etched the cobalt sky. You could feel on your face the gentle, unceasing wind. The silence there was profound. At night we gazed up at that narrow swath into a pitch black sky with stars close enough to touch—and the rest of the world seemed very far away.

The notion of canoeing is a seemingly simple one. But there is more here than meets the eye. In his book *The Lonely Land*, wilderness author Sigurd Olson describes well the sublime joys of canoeing—and their subtle impact on the soul:

"There is the feel of a paddle and the movement of a canoe, a magic compounded by distance, adventure, solitude and peace. The way of a canoe is the way of the wilderness and of a freedom almost forgotten, the open door to waterways of ages past and a way of life with profound and abiding satisfactions."

Checklists

DAY TRIPS
Canoe
Paddle
PFD
Helmet
Throw rope
Duct tape/repair kit
Small first-aid kit
Bailer (if necessary)
Lunch
Water bottle
Sunscreen
Spare clothing in waterproof bag
Waterproof bag
Rescue gear
River clothing suitable for conditions encountered
Footgear
Camera
Map, guidebook
Matches, fire starter
Toilet paper
Wallet and keys

OVERNIGHT TRIPS
Canoe
Paddle and spare

PFD
Helmet
Throw rope
Full repair kit
Full first-aid kit
Bailer (if necessary)
Water bottle
Sunscreen
River clothing suitable for conditions encountered
Footgear
Camp clothing
Camp shoes
Wallet and keys
Carabiner or pulleys for rescues
Waterproof bags and boxes
Tent or bivy shelter
Sleeping bag
Air mattress or pad
Food
Cookware and kitchen gear
Camp stove
Fuel
Flashlight
First-aid kit/emergency supplies (including space blankets)
Water containers
Firepan

Map, guidebook
Toilet paper
Plastic trowel, folding shovel, or
    toilet box
Insect repellent

Garbage bags
Signaling devices
Camera, fishing gear, etc.
Toiletries

APPENDIX 2

Canoe Manufacturers

American Traders Classic Canoes
627 Barton Rd.
Greenfield, MA 01301
413/773-9631

Atkinson Boat Co.
3258 E. Mullett Lk. Rd.
Indiana River, MI 49749
616/238-8825

Bear Creek Canoe, Inc.
RR 1, Box 1638, Rt. 11
Limerick, ME 04048
207/793-2005
Fax 207/793-4733

Bell Canoe Works
25355 Hwy. 169 South
Zimmerman, MN 55398
612/856-2231

Black Duck Boat Shop
143 West St.
New Milford, CT 06776
203/350-5170 #3

Blackhawk Canoe
1140 North Parker Dr.
Jonesville, WI 53545
608/754-2179

Bluegrass Canoes, Inc.
7323 Peaks Mill Rd.
Frankfort, KY 40601
502/227-4492
Fax 502/227-8086

Blue Hole Canoe Company
18079-B James Madison Hwy.
Gordonsville, VA 22942
540/832-7855
Fax 540/832-7854

Bluewater Canoes/Rockwood
Outfitters
699 Speedvale Ave. W
Guelph, Ontario N1K 1E6
Canada
519/824-1415
Fax 519/824-8750

Bourquin Boats
1568 McMahon Blvd.
Ely, MN 55731
218/365-5499

Bryan Boatbuilding
R.R. 3
St. George, New Brunswick
E0G 2Y0
Canada
506/755-2486

Burt's Canoes
Rt. 1, Box 1090
Litchfield, MO 04350
207/268-4802

Cal-Tek Engineering
36 Riverside Dr.
Kingston, MA 02364
617/585-5666

Camp Canoes
9 Averill
Otego, NY 13825
607/988-6842

Canoes by Whitewell Ltd.
2362 Dresden Dr.
Atlanta, GA 30341
404/325-5330

Cedarwood Canoes
Port Sanfield, RR#2
Port Carling, Ontario, P0B 1J0
Canada
705/765-6282

Chamcock Boat & Canoe
Glebe Rd., RR#2
St. Andrews, New Brunswick
E0G 2X0
Canada
506/529-4776

Chicagoland Canoe Base, Inc.
4109 N. Narragonsett Ave.
Chicago, IL 60634
312/777-1489

Curtis Canoe, Inc.
P.O. Box 750
Honeoye, NY 14471
716/229-5022
Fax 716/229-4723

Dagger Canoe Co.
P.O. Box 1500
Harriman, TN 37748
423/882-0404
Fax 423/882-8153

Dagger Composites
315 Roddy Ln.
Harriman, TN 37748
423/882-3547
Fax 423-882-8317

Easy Rider Canoe & Kayak Co.
P. O. Box 88108
Seattle, WA 98138
206/228-3633

Englehart Products, Inc.
P.O. Box 377
Newbury, OH 44065
216/564-5565
Fax 216/564-5515

Explorer Canoe Co.
P.O. Box 173
Lyndonville, VT 05851
802/626-8648
Fax 802/626-1157

Fletcher Canoes
Highway 11B, Box#1321
Aikokan, Ontario P0T 1C0
Canada
807/597-6801

Grasse River Boatworks
P.O. Box 496
Canton, NY 13617
315/386-1363

Great Canadian Canoe Co.
64 Worcester Providence Tpk.
(Rt. 146)
Sutton, MA 01590
508/865-0010
Fax 508/865-5220

Grumman Canoes
P.O. Box 549
Marathon, NY 13803
607/849-3211

Hemlock Canoe Works
P.O. Box 68
Hemlock, NY 14466-0068
716/367-3040

Hoefgen Canoes
N1927/Hwy. M-35
Menominee, MI 49858
906/863-3991
Fax 906/863-7754

Indian River Canoe Mfg.
4155 South St.
Titusville, FL 32780
407/267-7575

Jensen Canoes Research
308 78th Ave. N
Minneapolis, MN 55444
612/561-2229
473 N. Robin Hood Rd.
Inverness, FL 33450
904/344-0624

Karel's Fiberglass Products
789 Kailua Rd.
Kailua, HI 96734
Phone/Fax 808/261-8424

Kevin Martin, Boatbuilder
RFD 1, Box 441
Epping, NH 03042
603/679-5153

Kruger Ventures
2906 Meister Lane
Lansing, MI 48906
517/323-2139

Leisure Life Limited
4855 Broadmoor SE
Grand Rapids, MI 49512
616/698-3000
Fax 616/698-2734

Lincoln PaddleLite Canoes
RR2, Box 106
Freeport, ME 04032
207/865-0455

Mad River Canoe
P.O. Box 610
Waitsfield, VT 05673
802/496-3127
Fax 802/496-6247

Massive Outdoor Products
100 Hinchey Ave., Suite 517
Ottawa, Ontario K1Y 4L9
Canada
613/728-7931

McCurdy & Reed Canoes
RR2, Hampton Annapolis
Nova Scotia B0S 1L0
Canada
902/665-2435

Merrimack Canoe Co., Inc.
202 Harper Ave.
Crossville, TN 38555
615/484-4556
Fax 615/456-7918

Meyers Boat Company
343 Lawrence St.
Adrian, MI 49221
517/265-9821

Mid-Canada Fiberglass Ltd./Scott
Canoe Co.
Box 1599
New Liskeard, Ontario P0J 1P0
Canada
705/647-6548
Fax 705/647-6698

Middle Path Boats
Box 8881
Pittsburgh, PA 15221
412/247-4860

Millbrook Boats
49 Lufkin Rd.
Weare, NH 03281
Phone/Fax 603/529-3919

Miller Canoes
RR#1 Nictau
Plaster Rock, New Brunswick
E0J 1W0
Canada
506/356-2409
Fax 506/356-2580

Mohawk Canoes
963 N CR 427
Longwood, FL 32750
407/834-3233
Fax 407/834-0292

Monfort Associates
RR2, Box 416
Wiscosset, ME 04578-9610
207/882-5504

Moore Canoes
3 Cardinal Court
Hilton Head Island, SC 29926
803/681-5986
Fax 803/681-3650

Morley Cedar Canoes
P.O. Box 5147
Swan Lake, MT 59911
406/886-2242

Muskoka Fine Watercraft &
Supply Company Limited
24 Brock Street West
Uxbridge, Ontario L9P 1P3
Canada
905/731-8295
Fax 905/731-0197

Nature Bound Canoe
Rt. 140, 93 Gardner Rd.
Winchendon, MA 01475
508/297-0288

Navarro Canoe Co.
199 Rogue River Pkwy.
Talent, OR 97540
541/512-9447
Fax 541/512-9448

New River Canoe Mfg., Inc.
Rt. 2, Box 575
Independence, VA 24348
703/773-3124

Nova Craft Canoes Ltd.
4389 Exeter Rd.
London, Ontario N6L 1A4,
Canada
519/652-3649
Fax 519/652-6803

Old Town Canoe Co.
58 Middle St.
Old Town, ME 04468
207/827-5513
Fax 207/827-2779

Pakboats
P.O. Box 700
Enfield, NH 03748
603/632-7654
Fax 603/632-5611

Patrick Moore Canoeing
P.O. Box 242
Stoughton, WI 53589
608/873-5989

Phoenix Poke Boats, Inc.
P.O. Box 109
207 North Broadway
Berea, KY 40403
606/986-2336
Fax 606/986-3277

Porta-Bote International
1074 Independence Ave.
Mountain View, CA 94043
800/227-8882

Prijon/Wildwasser Sport USA,
Inc.
P.O. Box 4617
Boulder, CO 80306
303/444-2336
Fax 303/444-2375

Radisson Products
P.O. Box 130
Callander, Ontario P0H 1H0
Canada
612/476-2766

Red River Canoe & Paddle
63 Ellesmere Ave.
Winnipeg, Manitoba R2M 0G4
Canada
204/878-2524

Riverjammer Canoe Co.
191 Crawley Falls Rd.
Brentwood, NH 03833
Phone/Fax 603/642-8522

Ruch Canoes
Minett Post Office
Muskoka, Ontario P0B 1G0
Canada
705/765-5390

Sawyer Canoe Company
234 S. State St.
Oscoda, MI 48750
517/739-9181

Souris River Canoes
104 Reid St., Box 1116
Atikokan, Ontario P0T 1C0
Canada
807/597-1292
Fax 807/597-5871

Spencer Canoes
Rt. 1, Box 55R
Martindale, TX 78655
512/357-6113

Stewart River Boatworks
Rt. 1, Box 2038
Two Harbors, MN 55616
218/834-5037

Swift Canoe & Kayak Company
RR 1, Oxtongue Lake
Dwight, Ontario P0A 1H0
Canada
705/635-1167
Fax 705/635-1834

Temagami Canoe Company
P.O. Box 520
Temagami, Ontario P0H 2H0,
Canada
705/569-3777

Tender Craft Boat Shop, Inc.
284 Brock Ave.
Toronto, Ontario MK6 2M4
Canada
416/531-2941
Fax 416/323-0992

Three Rivers Canoe Co.
P.O. Box 173
Lyndonville, VT 05851
802/626-8648
Fax 802/626-1157

Trailhead
1960 Scott St.
Ottawa, Ontario K1Z 8L8
Canada
613/722-4229
Fax 613/722-0245

Vermont Canoe Products
RR1, Box 353A
Newport, VT 05855
802/754-2307

We-no-nah Canoe, Inc.
P.O. Box 247
Winona, MN 55987
507/454-5430
Fax 507/454-5448

West Coast Canoe Company
P.O. Box 143
Campbell River, British Columbia
V9W 5A7
Canada
800/446-1588
Fax 250/287-3962

Western Canoeing Manufacturing,
Inc.
Box 115
Abbotsford, British Columbia
V2S 4N8
Canada
604/853-9320
Fax 604/852-6933

Woodstrip Watercraft Co.
1818 Swamp Pike
Gilbertsville, PA 19525
610/326-9282

Equipment Sources

Carlisle Paddles, Inc.
P.O. Box 488
Grayling, MI 49738
800/258-0290
517/348-9886

Cascade Outfitters
P.O. Box 209
Springfield, OR 97477
800/223-7238
503/747-2272

Colorado Kayak Supply
P.O. Box 3059
Buena Vista, CO 81211
800/535-3565
719/395-2422
Fax 719/395-2421

Down River Equipment
12100 West Sand Avenue
Wheat Ridge, CO 80033
303/467-9489
Fax 303/940-8812

Four Corners River Sports
P.O. Box 379
Durango, CO 81302
800/426-7637
970/259-3893
Fax 970/247-7819

NOC Outfitter's Store
13077 Hwy. 19 West
Bryson City, NC 28713
800/367-3521
704/488-6737
Fax 704/488-8039

Northwest River Supplies
2009 South Maine
Moscow, ID 83843
800/635-5202
208/882-2383
Fax 208/883-4787

Wildwater Designs
230 Penllyn Pike
Penllyn, PA 19422
215/646-5034

Wyoming River Raiders
601 Wyoming Boulevard
Casper, WY 82609
800/247-6068
307/235-8624

APPENDIX 4

Canoe Camping Supplies

L.L. Bean, Inc.
Freeport, ME 04033
800/221-4221

Duluth Tent & Awning, Inc.
P.O. Box 16024
Duluth, MN 55816-0024
800/777-4439

NOC Outfitter's Store
13077 Hwy. 19 West
Bryson City, NC 28713-9114
800/367-3521

Piragis Northwoods Company
105 North Central Avenue
Ely, MN 55731
800/223-6565

Recreational Equipment, Inc.
1700 45th Street East
Sumner, WA 98390
800/426-4840

APPENDIX 5

Periodicals

American Whitewater
American Whitewater Association
P.O. Box 85
Phoenicia, NY 12464

Canoe & Kayak
Canoe America Associates
P.O. Box 3146
Kirkland, WA 98083
800/692-2663
206/827-6363
Fax 206/827-1893

Currents
National Organization for River
Sports
P.O. Box 6847
Colorado Springs, CO 80904
719/473-2466

Paddler
American Canoe Association
(ACA)
7432 Alban Station Road
Suite B-226
Springfield, VA 22150
703/451-0141

APPENDIX 6

Conservation Organizations

America Canoe Association (ACA)
7432 Alban Station Road
Suite B-226
Springfield, VA 22150
703/451-0141

American Rivers
801 Pennsylvania Ave. S.E.
Suite 400
Washington, DC 20003
202/547-6900

American Whitewater Affiliation
(ANA)
136 13th Street S.E.
Washington, DC 20003
202/546-3766

Friends of the River (FOR)
909 12th Street, Suite 207
Sacramento, CA 95814
916/442-3155

National Organization for River
Sports (NORS)
P.O. Box 6847
Colorado Springs, CO 80904
719/473-2466

The River Conservation Fund
323 Pennsylvania Ave. N.E.
Washington, DC 20003
202/547-6900

United States Canoe Association
606 Ross St.
Middletown, OH 45044
513/422-3739

GLOSSARY

Big water. Rivers with large volumes and powerful hydraulics

Boulder garden. Rapids densely strewn with boulders

Brace. A paddle stroke used to prevent the canoe from flipping over

Breaking wave. A standing wave that falls upstream

Cfs. Cubic feet per second; a measurement of the volume of water flowing past a given point per second

Chute. A narrow, constricted portion of the river

Cushion. A pillow (see below)

Draw stroke. Sideways pull of the paddle toward the canoe

Eddy. An area in the river where the current either stops or moves upstream opposite the main current; usually found below obstructions and on the inside of bends

Eddy line. The sharp boundary between two currents of different velocity or direction, usually marked by swirling water and bubbles

Feather. To turn the blade of a paddle horizontal to the water

Ferry. A maneuver for moving a boat laterally across the current

Gradient. The slope of a riverbed, usually expressed in the number of feet per mile the river drops

Haystack. A large, unstable standing wave

Hole. See *reversal*

Hypothermia. The serious medical condition caused by the lowering of body temperature, requiring immediate first aid

Keeper. A large hole or reversal that can hold a swimmer for a long time

Lining. Guiding the boat downstream from the shore with ropes to avoid running rapids

Pillow. A cushion of water that forms on the upstream side of rocks or other obstacles

Pool-and-drop. A river with intermittent rapids followed by long sections of calm water

Portage. To carry boats and equipment around rapids

Pry stroke. Sideways push of the paddle away from the canoe

Put-in. The beginning point of a river trip

Reversal. An area of the river where the current turns upstream and revolves back on itself, forming a treacherous current requiring caution; often called hydraulics, stoppers, keepers, curlers, and holes

Riffle. Shallow, gentle rapids

Roller. A big curling wave that falls back upstream on itself

Roostertail. An explosion of spray from water hitting a rock or other obstacle

Scout. To examine rapids from shore

Standing wave. A high wave caused by the slowing of the current

Stern rudder. A corrective stroke where the paddle is used as a rudder to correct inadvertent veering of the canoe

Stopper. A hole or breaking wave capable of stopping or flipping boats

Strainer. Exposed rocks, usually on the outside of a bend, presenting a hazard to boaters

Sweeper. Fallen tree or brush that lies in the path of the current

Tailwave. Standing wave that forms at the base of rapids

Take-out. The ending point of a river trip

Technical. A river with many obstacles that requires constant maneuvering

Tongue. The smooth V of fast water found at the head of rapids, usually indicating the deepest and least obstructed channel

Undercut. A rock or ledge with water flowing underneath it

Wave train. A series of standing waves

Wrapping. The partial submersion that occurs when a boat's upstream side becomes lodged underwater against a boulder